Discipline in Family Resource Management

It Works!
Biblical Theory
Budget Planning
Personal Testimony

By Viola L. Britt
As Inspired by
the Holy Spirit

Discipline in Family Resource Management
Viola L. Britt
ISBN # 0-89228-132-4

Published for the author by
Impact Christian Books, Inc.
332 Leffingwell Ave.
Kirkwood, MO 63122
314-822-3309

*All scripture quotations are taken from the
Authorized King James Version
of the Bible, unless otherwise stated.*

In Dedication

first,

To my ever present Lord & Savior,
Holy Jesus Christ
Who promoted me to the rank of a scribe
that I might say, "Yes, LORD!"
to His call to pen the words
that He dictated to my spirit as I wrote.

"...my tongue is the pen of a ready writer."
Psalm 45:1

---

second,

To my Pastors
Norbert and Daisy Simmons
of
Deeper Life Church Ministries
for their serene support
in the press of much spiritual warfare

In Gratitude

I am forever grateful to my dear mom,
Verniece,
for all her support
in supplying my administrative needs
in getting the manuscript ready for publication.

———————————

For their unswerving commitment to excellence
in their professional support of draft reviews,
I am forever grateful to
Nora Jean Harper, my sister,
and
Margaret Holman, my sister in the Lord

———————————

Thanks *James and Gala*
for making the Budget work!

TABLE OF CONTENTS

REFERENCES

FOREWORD

When the book *Raising Responsible Children In A Single Parent Home* appeared on the market in the fall of 1997, many people - single parents, married parents, and even single individuals - saw such benefit from the resource management emphasis made in almost every chapter that it sparked the beginning of many resource management seminars in our geographical area. These seminars brought out interesting discoveries about the root of many financial problems in family budgeting as personal budget plans were set up in accordance with what the Word of God says about our stewardship as Christians.

The LORD led me to delve deeper into the root of the problems people had managing their finances. He revealed financial sins, curses, ignorances and other imbalances in decision making related to flesh versus spirit motivations. Many homes were so supernaturally blessed by the discipline that followed that the need for such a publication as this was generated.

Although the material for these seminars originated from the parenting book, the inspirational knowledge which surfaced is an unveiling that is to be shared with all Christians.

author

The contents of this book are intriguing, concise and beneficial if applied appropriately. We must be doers of the Word and not hearers and readers only. No application, no results; and if we are to achieve whatsoever we desire to have, each individual must press, and strive to endure hardships and setbacks. If applied correctly, and then letting patience have her perfect work, the reader will obtain true prosperity and have financial success. This book will let people know that they don't have to play lotteries, gamble, sell drugs, con, cheat, steal or commit any henious crimes to obtain wealth, but they can apply the Word of God and have great success. My wife and I have known Viola Britt for the past several years. We have witnessed that the accounts of her personal testimony in this book attest to true success in financial management.

Minister Carl Holman
McKenney, Virginia

Viola Britt writes from a deep experience in her walk with God. She has walked the walk. She has put into practice the deep things of God she has gleaned from a disciplined daily study of God's Word and a prayer life that has sought after God's own heart. She has dared to trust God in the raising of her children and in the stewardship of finances and she has found Him faithful. This is not a theological study but a testimony to the foundational truth to be found in God's Word and the reality of that truth demonstrated in daily living.

Jesus is indeed, the Way, the Truth and the Life and Viola is an eloquent witness. To God be the glory.

Roy Mendelsohn
Cincinnati, Ohio

PREFACE

Every successful business that has every succeeded financially in this Country has had in its operation biblical principles that worked because they were originally set in place by God. It doesn't matter even if that businessman isn't a Christian. Biblical financial management principles work for whoever uses them.

Many young businessmen who have become heirs of wealthy old family business empires don't even realize how their great, great, great grandparents applied prosperity principles from the Holy Bible, the main book they put their trust in in those days. Many of these deceased business tycoons amassed an insurmountable fortune and passed it down from generation to generation of offsprings who would dare not touch ole' grandpa's business management procedures because they were what made the business thrive. (Oh, Yes, they probably bought new furniture and upgraded equipment and bookkeeping techniques but they left the basic business management concept in tact.)

Later, the younger generations even amassed more wealth by publishing books on what their grandpa did to become so successful, that others may read, learn and know about smart ole' grandpa while the inheriting youngsters just basked in the accolades that came from what grandpa originally got from the Word of God. Little did they know that the pin-pointing of the true origin was actually lost because all emphasis was placed on that witty business head of ole' grandpa, the wisest businesman you ever met!

In recent years, the church has taken a positive step toward educating Christians on successful financial resource management techniques, taking the concepts that have proven to work in the world system and adding scriptural significance through pin-pointing the where-abouts of these principles in the Holy Bible. This is obviously a good conscientious start; however, considering the fact that the world system's package has "white-washed" the spiritual origins of many financial shortcomings from what it has to teach us, we need to do more than just locate these financial scriptures in the Bible and tack them on to what the world system already knows about financial management. Instead, we need to reach back further beyond what the world system has to show us to get to the root of recurring financial crises which we seem to not be able to resolve by just taking on a second job, a higher paying job, debt consolidation, budgeting, saving and other natural resourceful avenues.

This is why this book deals, upfront, with spiritual breaches we have made against God in applying His Word in our lifestyles that have brought us into financial sins, under financial curses, out from under proper financial coverings, and into just plain ignorance that have caused us to misappropriate God's money. Not until we've properly studied these points, repented of these sins, changed our actions and provided necessary restitution, can we even begin to think about planning and living by a scripturally based budget plan.

It is with this serious burden in my spirit that God has led me to lay out, under one cover, His spiritual and natural disciplines in successful family resource management. We are accountable to God to pass down His will on stewardship of His financial resources to our children, *"that the generation to come might know them, even the children which should be born; who should arise and declare them to their children: that they might set their hope in God, and not forget the works of God, but keep His commandments."*   *(Psalm 78:5-7)*

If you are really serious about lining up your immediate family's and church families financial spending habits with the Word of God, I challenge you to set up training sessions with the transparency masters provided in Appendix G. These transparency masters can be used in any group setting in church, at home, on your job and even in your community to spread the word about God's foundational principles on money management.

The Lord Jesus admonished Peter that to show his love for Him he must *"feed my lambs"* (referring to individual, one-on-one nurturing) and *"feed my sheep"* (referring to the nurture of a group, as a congregational setting). I too heed the call to nurture the flock of God and pray that any Christian leader that picks up this book also picks up this spirit of obedience to the commission our Lord Jesus gave to all who are true disciples of Christ.

*"...Did not our heart burn
within us ..... while He
opened to us the Scriptures? "*

---

*"Then opened He
their understanding
that they might
understand the Scriptures"*

(St. Luke 24: 32, 45)

PART I:

WHAT THE BIBLE SAYS ABOUT FINANCES THAT THE CHURCH HAS FORGOTTEN

1. The Spirituality of Money

2. Financial Sins

3. Financial Vows & Pledges

4. Financial Curses

5. Financial Ignorances

6. Financial Coverings

7. Association With Prosperous People

8. Learning To Give

9. Wisdom From Solomon On Handling Finances

10. Trusting God To Meet Your Needs

§

CHAPTER 1

THE SPIRITUALITY OF MONEY

PRINCIPLES OF BIBLICALLY BASED FINANCIAL MANAGEMENT

When you look at God's arithmetic formula for the return on the dollar when you give to kingdom work versus that of the interest rate method used by banking and investment institutions there is no conceivable way of getting around the fact that God's process of financial return far outweighs that of the world system. Yet, you must qualify for such spiritual returns on your dollar.

The ministry emphasis of this book is to get you to a place in accountability, desire and lifestyle where you can actually experience such returns on the monetary resources and material possessions which God has entrusted to you. Yes, God wants us to be content with the basics of life. But this contentment is based on bringing us back under the umbrella of trust in Him, alone, to use us as a channel through which He can resourcefully propel ministry work throughout the world.   When we've arrived at that point in our thinking and financial accountability, the Lord will begin to make the concept of "living on the basics" in our lives reach another dimension of victorious living. He will bring our lives in line with His will so much so that our desires in making personal purchases, obligations and general household budget plans will always include generous giving to church ministry, the poor and any other kingdom work God presents to us. He wants us to no longer think that just the tithe (10%) is His. God wants us to realize that He is holding us accountable for every dime of the 10% tithe and the 90% that He has entrusted to our stewardship as managers of that which belongs to Him.

The Lord has great heavenly riches which He wants to release to your trustworthy stewardship and management. Just listen to the spiritual anointing He can place on your finances as these Scriptures speak to your spirit:

"And I will give thee the treasures of darkness, and hidden riches of secret places..." (Isaiah 45:3)

" And everyone that hath forsaken houses, or brethren, or sisters, or father, or mother, or wife, or children ....for my name's sake, shall receive an hundredfold, and shall inherit everlasting life." (Matt 19:29)

"And other fell on good ground, and ..... brought forth some thirty, and some sixty, and some an hundredfold." (Mk 4:8)

Do you know where the hidden riches of secret places are?

Do you know what the treasures of darkness are?

Do you know how much 30, 60, and 100 fold amount to in the financial return on your dollar?

Would you get the same return on your money if you invested it in the world system?

These are questions that neither your banker, investment counselor, nor financial manager would spend the time in attempting to answer because these promises are based on a spiritual seeding, incubation, and multiplication process. Yet to keep your focus balanced, listen to the flip side of these promises for there is such a   thing as "spiritual consumption" that could deteriorate the value of your financial profile when you're walking outside the will and statutes of God in your financial stewardship:

"...riches certainly make themselves wings; they fly away as an eagle toward heaven." (Prov 23:5)

"Ye have sown much, and bring in little ....he that earneth wages earneth wages to put it into a bag with holes." (Haggai 1:6)

"...An evil ....common among men: A man ....hath .....riches, wealth, and honour, ...yet ....a stranger eateth it .....this is .....an evil disease." (Eccles 6:1-2)

Your actions will determine whether your finances will be consumed or multiplied.

CONSUMPTION VERSUS MULTIPLICATION

Our financial profiles will fall in either one or the other spiritually controlled category, consumption or multiplication, based on our management or mismanagement of that which belongs to God. I never even considered this spiritual side of money until the day the Lord spoke to me, *"Viola, a dollar bill will never be the same in your hand again; it will be whatever you'll need it to be when a financial need arises."* Little did I know, then, that I could literally throw away my calculator, for then, I had entered God's manifold

"Investment Returns: Kingdom vs World System"	
Kingdom	
When you invest in Kingdom work, God's return on the dollar is:	Percentage Rates
double what you put in (= x2 of principal)	200%
30 fold of what you put in (= x30 of prin)	3,000%
60 fold of what you put in (= x60 of prin)	6,000%
100 fold of what you put in (= x100 of prin)	10,000%
World System	
When you invest in the world system, i.e. savings, CD's, mutual funds, variable insurances, treasury notes, etc., the world system's return on the dollar is:	
a % of what you put in (=.024 of principal)	2.4%
a % of what you put in (=.067 of principal)	6.7%
a % of what you put in (=.12 of principal)	12%
a % of what you put in (=.21 of principal)	21%

Christians have within our power the possibility to control the entire financial system of this earth, yet we go for the "bread crumbs" (immediate satisfaction, that which we can see and check on every day) over the supernatural multiplication process of trusting in and waiting on God.

blessings which could not be mathematically tracked based on the world's invest-ment return formulas or the amount of ministry seed I had planted. The Lord literally carried me to another dimension in my thinking about the spirit behind the monetary system. I use to think money was all carnal because it's what makes the world system operate. When I got a handle on the truth, which is found in God's Word, I literally put every point to the test of "do or die" and every time God lifted me out of situations that I would not even had believed were possible unless I had been there to see it with my own eyes!

Ladies and Gentlemen, boys and girls, if you've experienced any of the above "spiritual consumptions" in your resources, whether liquidated funds or material items, you will be enriched from the wisdom you will receive from this book in applying God's financial principles to that which He has given you to manage. It's all in the Word of God; It's just time for the blinders to come off. And the anointing on this book will do just that for you as you purpose in your heart to become a hearer of this fruitful word imparted by the Holy Spirit.

God only gives spiritual prosperity to stewards. With His will in your spirit, He will put His prosperity in your hand. Now let's learn how to avoid financial sins, curses, and ignorances; how to recognize and come out of satanic captivity in financial strongholds; and how to and operate under the protections of God's ordained financial coverings.

DOES GOD WANT YOU TO HAVE MATERIAL POSSESSIONS?
YES!

Abraham had possessions:

"And he said, I am Abraham's servant. And the Lord hath blessed my master greatly.......and He hath given him flocks, and herds, and silver, and gold, and menservants.... maidservants, and camels, and asses." (Gen 24:35)

The early Christians had possessions:

"And sold their possessions and goods, and parted them to all...had need." (Acts 2:45)

DOES GOD WANT YOU TO HAVE MONEY AND PROSPER?
YES!

Joseph prospered:

"And the LORD was with Joseph, and he was a prosperous man . ...the LORD made all that he did to prosper in his hand." (Gen 39:2-3)

God has already pronounced prosperity on us:

".....he that soweth bountifully shall reap also bountifully." (II Cor 9:6b)

People have always used money as legal tender and the World has always operated on a monetary system:

"And Joseph gathered all the money that was found in the land of Egypt ......and Joseph brought all the money into Pharaoh's house." (Gen 47:14)

Monetary systems are God based that we might be accountable to someone else on earth who is likewise accountable to Him, regardless of their acknowledgement of Him as Supremely God:

"Thus saith Cyrus king of Persia, All the kingdoms of the earth hath the LORD God of heaven given me; and He hath charged me to build Him a house in Jerusalem....." *(II Chron 36:23, Ezra 1:2)*

GOD's PURPOSES FOR YOUR FINANCES

To establish covenants between you and God --

".....It is He that giveth thee power to get wealth, to establish covenant." *(Deu 8:18)*

To finance the LORD's ministry work --

"Bring ye all the tithes...(and offerings, vs8) into the storehouse, that there may be meat in my house..." *(Mal 3:10)*

To allow God's spiritual prosperity to manifest through a natural source --

"I will...open you the windows of heaven, and pour you out a blessing...I will rebuke the devourer." *(Mal 3:10-11)*

To Give to the Needy (saints and evangelized non-saints) --
"...let him labour...that he may have to give to him that needeth." (Eph 4:28)

To Meet Your Family's Daily Needs --
"....having food and raiment...be...content." (I Tim 6:8)
"Take therefore no thought for the morrow..." (Matt 6:34)

Just as God has divine purposes for your finances so, adversely, Satan has purposed to hinder you from reaping benefit from following God's divine purposes. Take a moment to consider this very important financial point, pictorially:

YOUR FINANCES

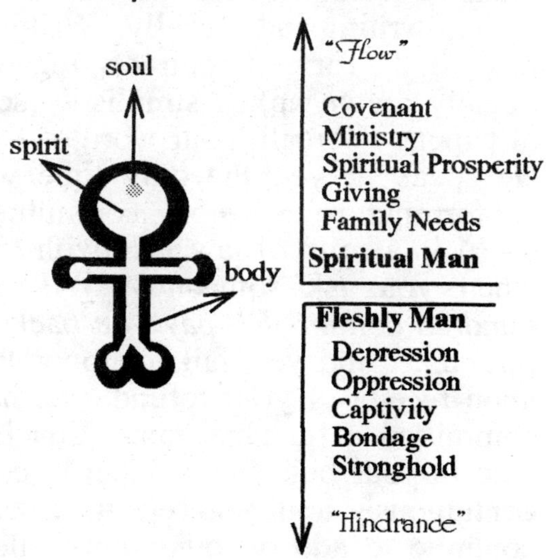

God wants to impart spiritual wisdom to your **spirit** via the Holy Spirit that you might receive knowledge and understanding in your **mind** to apply, naturally, what the **body** should do, physically, with His money. Prov 2:10

SATAN'S PURPOSES AGAINST

However, Satan does not come and overtake us against our own free will. Depending on where we are spiritually with the LORD, we will either follow God's divine plan, through our spirit, or follow the way of the flesh (body), the part of us that Satan can and will use.

Even as Christians, we can sometimes follow the way of the flesh in financial dealings that will cause us to commit sins and ignorances and bring curses upon our finances because of spiritual holes we have wedged in our God-given hedges -- holes which Satan's evil spirits wiggle through and BITE:

"...whoso breaketh a hedge, a serpent shall bite him." (Eccles 10:8b)

We will now take a closer look at these financial vices in light of the Word of God.

THE SEAL OF FINANCIAL COMMITMENTS

It seems to be a forgotten truth, today, that financial commitments are still sealed in two ways: both in writing and verbally. Written commitments are made in the form of contracts, regardless how complex (legally drawn up) or simplistic (scribbled on a piece of paper). Verbally, our word of honor is given when we speak it; yet, the only time we still see people conforming to a verbal commitment is when they swear in a court of law. Notwithstanding, even today, when you ask someone, *"Will you loan me one hundred dollars? I'll pay you back when I get my tax refund..."*, and you fail to honor that verbal promise upon receipt of your refund, you have lied; you have committed a financial sin. You have just opened a hole in your budget for Satan to come in and devour, continuously until you repent. Even worse, when you continue to add on other unfulfilled, half-considered verbal commitments, *"I'm sorry I put that dent in your car; I'll get it fixed payday..."*, as casual as they may seem to you, Satan's devouring of your finances will become so diseased that you won't know where to start to seal these unseen spiritual holes.

FINANCIAL HOLES

*"But this is a people robbed .....snared in holes, and
they are hid in prison houses: they are a prey and
none delivereth; for a spoil and none saith, Restore!"*
(Isaiah 42:22)

After we have breached financial commitments,
many times we'll try to patch up that hole because it
looks like a little one but we usually find that it has
become infected. However, once we go back and deal
with the breach, we'll begin to see it mend.

Understanding Financial Holes. Let's spend a
few moments in studying just how these spiritual holes
occur to observe how Satan operates to cause us to fall
out of the perfect will of God concerning the
management of His finances. It is very important to
see that WE are the culprits, not Satan, for when we
walk outside of God's will, we make that wrong move
he wants us to make to cause us to give him legal
ground, now, to do his job of depressing and oppressing our finances, bringing them into varying degrees of
captivity, bondage and eventually strongholds. His
area of play is limited, though; he can only oppress
where we refuse to bring our finances in line with
God's will. We must first be operating in the flesh,
then we must choose one of two avenues, Restoration
or Degeneration:

➡ RESTORATION
   Repent → correct sin → restore Christ's covering → pinhole mended

➡ DEGENERATION
   Don't repent → coverup, → attract spirits → cancerous hole enlarges
            ignore   of consumption

It's only when we've walked in the flesh for a
period of time that we've opened up ground to satanic
influence. We've opened the ground; he's just doing

his job,
> *"The thief cometh not, but for to steal, and to kill, and to destroy..." (John 10:10a)*

Understanding the Spiritual Response to Our Natural Actions. Because God is a God of order He has established His creation to automatically function on pre-established conditions that He has already set in place from the very beginning of time. Satan knows that he must submit to God's order, so adversely, he leads a troop of demonic forces in ranking order, in negation or retroflex to God's order (Eph 6:12). Thus, when we execute certain actions it causes certain other reactions to occur in the spiritual realm --cause and effect-- thusly, if that action we choose is in contrast to God's will, the reaction will be adverse, and adverse actions are executed by adversaries. However, Great News!!! God has anointed Jesus Christ with the Holy Ghost and with power to heal our sick finances when they are oppressed of the devil. (Acts 10:38)

Unwitting Assistance To Family And Friends. Let's not forget that all individuals in our blood relations, in our community, and on the job are not followers of Christ. Although they may help one another, financially, and there seems to result no adverse reaction in the spiritual realm, when we provide financial assistance to those same individuals, under certain circumstances, Satan considers and marks our steps because we are already marked, "saints...believers...Christians...seal of God in our foreheads (potential)..."; therefore, any mercies he may show to two other individuals who serve him well, he will not show to you; so, you must be leary of even what you may consider to be a trite financial benevolence that you feel God will bless:

     • Earning part-time money from someone else, freeing them up to do something out of God's will (i.e., babysitting for an unmarried couple while they go out of town on a vacation, babysitting for another person who's working a 2nd or 3rd job out of God's will, etc.).

• Loaning people money that allows them to go do something out of the will of God or that indirectly supports ungodly ends (i.e., money used by a youth to buy secular music and its equipment, a silent partnership in a business venture that involves the selling of tobacco products, alcoholic beverages, etc.).

I'm not saying to never loan your family or acquaintenances money or assist their logistical needs. Just be cognizant. Ask questions, "Where are you going?...Why do you need the money?..." If they can't answer you or feel that it's none of your business, then don't use God's money or time to get involved in any of their business. **There is a difference between money and services provided to non-Christians which is "ministry oriented" and which is "ministry hindering". Just make sure your assistance is "ministry oriented."**

Also consider that any part-time, evening and weekend second-income work that you are involved in, yourself, may also be interfering with God's divine will in your life. Go to God, in prayer, to determine the source of your financial hole before trying to mend it through unprofitable means.

CHAPTER 2

FINANCIAL SINS

FINANCIAL SINS: THE ENEMY OF PROSPERITY

Financial sins hinder us from enjoying God's prosperity:

".....Thus saith God, Why transgress ye the commandments of the LORD, that ye can not prosper? Because ye have forsaken the LORD, He hath also forsaken you." (II Chronicles 24:20)

The sad thing about financial sins is that many times we are not aware that we are committing a sin; yet, this ignorance is treated, in the spiritual realm, just as a policeman would treat you, when stopped for speeding, and you say, *"Oh, I didn't know I was exceeding the speed limit, officer"* -- you still get charged with a fine.

Our financial transgressions can be lumped into three major categories -- Committed Sins, Sins of Omission and Sins of Ingratitude:

Committed Sins ➤ Unkept Vows -- Deu 23:21-23
Unkept Pledges -- Ezek 18:10-18
Self Inflicted Curses -- (Includes
tithes and offerings, etc) --
Mal 3:8-9, Jer 17:5
Unintentional Sin Committed Out of
Ignorance -- Lev 4
Misplaced Coverings --Isaiah 4:1,
I Cor 11:1-10
Presumptuous Sins -- Psalm 19:13
Bribes -- Psalms 26:9-10, I Sam 8:3
Transgressions of the Conscience
• Not Paying Poor Persons
You Owe -- Dan 24:14-15
• Not Forgiving Others Who

Owe You When You Have
Greater Unpaid Debt -- Matt
18:21-35
• Unequal Yoke Between
Two Believers -- II Cor 6:14

Sins of Omission ➤ Financial Actions, Directed By God,
Omitted By Us -- Deut
28:45, 62

Sins of Ingratitude ➤ Destruction of Someone Else's
Property or Gift To You Out
of Malice, Vice -- Includes
Misuse, Unuse, and Abuse of
Inheritance Gained Out of
Someone Else's Labor --
Prov 14:34, 17:2, 19:26

Committing any of the above sins will withhold blessings from you (Jeremiah 5:25; Ezekiel 44:30). We're going to look at these points closely in this book. Chapters follow which will address Vows, Pledges, Curses, Ignorance and Coverings. Presumptuous sin is addressed under *Settling Court-Ordered Financial Judgements* in Chapter 13. Adequate understanding of all other transgressions given above can be gained from reading the Scriptures listed.

WHAT CAUSES US TO COMMIT FINANCIAL SINS?

The Love of Money. *"For the love of money is the root of all evil..." (I Tim 6:10).* The Bible clearly tells us that we can not serve God and mammon for we will either hate the one and love the other. With the merging of the modern day Christian lifestyle with the mores of the world, particularly in America, we have learned to hate the ways of God (waiting, patience, trust......) and love mammon (instant money, credit, possessions...).

The love of money is a gross abominable sin because it leads us into spiritual whoredom. Spiritual whoredom is actually spiritual adultery against God -- being given over to idolatry; appearing to serve God yet worshiping that which fuels the world system, money. Well, what does God think about spiritual adultery? Is it as bad as physical adultery or not that important to Him?

When the Lord compared Israel and Judah to two daughters called Aholah and Aholibah, He told Ezekiel to judge them and declare unto them their abomination. They had committed adultery with their idols, blood was on their hands, and they had defiled His sanctuary by their very presence (Ezekiel 23:36-39). The Lord had the prophet Hosea marry a natural harlot named Gomer to show Israel, naturally, what they were doing to Him, spiritually, by looking to other gods. God called it a spirit of whoredom and that as a result of their spiritual whoredoms He would give them over to commit natural whoredoms. Here, you see that physical adultery is an outgrowth of spiritual adultery. This means a person committing natural adultery has already changed his gods (Hosea 4:12-18). Here, you can see how the love of money is tied in with the seeding of adultery, fornication, divorce, prostitution, abortion, and other sins of the body. This idolatrous worshiping of money and turning from God is so poignantly illustrated in these clips of Scripture:

*" But thou didst trust in thine own beauty, and playedst the harlot .....Thou hast also taken thy fair jewels of my **gold** and of my **silver** .....and madest to thyself **images of men**, and didst commit whoredom with them..." (Ezekiel 16:15-17).*

(Ezekiel 16 refers to this horrid idolatry as *"whoredom, harlotry, and nakedness"* 23 times!)

*"Their idols are **silver** and **gold**, the work of men's hands. They have mouths, but they speak not: eyes have they, but they see not: They have ears, but they hear not: noses have they, but they smell not: They have hands, but they handle not: feet have they, but they walk not: neither speak they through their throat. They that make them are like unto them; so is every one that trusteth in them." (Psalm 115:4-8, 135:15-18)*

Spiritual whoredom is so adulterous that it causes us to not reverence God as the one and only God in our lives; it causes us not to Rest in the Lord.

The Love of Money and The Breaking of The Sabbath. Because we have access to money, we have acquired the means to not honor one weekly "Day of Rest" for ourselves and for others to worship the Lord corporately; rest in Him intimately among family, relatives, and friends; and spend quality time quietly and richly meditating on His Word, personally.

The Lord Jesus Christ even acknowledged God's commandments as being, *"...thou shalt love the Lord thy **God** with **all** thy heart... soul... mind... strength... first commandment. And the second... Thou shalt love thy **neighbor** as thyself. There is none other commandment greater than these"* (Mark 12:30-31). These two commandments are a clear summation of the ten given in Exodus 20:

Old Testament		New Testament		Dealing With
Commandments 1-4	=	First Commandment	=	Sins Against God
Commandments 5-10	=	Second Commandment	=	Sins Against Man

Jesus did not delete the commandment to rest on the sabbath (#4) for in resting, we reverence God, not man. Nor did His disciples forsake honoring that Day of Rest even after Jesus had departed from this earth, for they, too, *"...rested the sabbath day according to the commandment"* (Luke 23:56). Yet, because we have access to money, God's money, through its power to gain access to earthly pursuits and pleasures, we have used it as legal tender to not acknowledge the Lord's Day of Rest.

The Love of Money and the Blue Law. In the earlier years of this Country, the majority of people were professing Christians. They made decisions on matters relating to family matters, education, and politics according to the Word of God. The family ate together, daily, with the children reciting Bible verses before eating; the school day started with Devotion and prayer; political leaders reverenced the Word of God in their speeches to the public and in defining the terms of constitutional rights:

"Of all the habits and dispositions which lead to political prosperity, religion and morality are indispensible supports. In vain would that man claim the tribute of patriotism who should labor to subvert these great pillars." **President George Washington***

"Sir, my concern is not whether God is on our side. My great concern is to be on God's side..."
President Abraham Lincoln*

"It can not be emphasized enough too strongly or too often that this great nation was founded not by religionists, but by Christians, not on religion but on the gospel of Jesus Christ."
The Honorable Patrick Henry*

Even if we re-incorporated Devotion and prayer into the public schools once again, it would never be the same as it was before prayer was banned because everyone would now be praying to different gods.

*Barton, David. *America's Godly Heritage,* Aledo, Texas, Wallbuilders, 1990

Many Christians blame the passing of Blue Laws for the tremendous increase in businesses operating on Sundays. However, in actuality, if we truly reverenced the Lord enough to keep one day as a holy rest day from all humanly initiated labor, we would have never let the passing of a government law regulate how we would spend what we call our free time on Sundays or whatever day you choose to set aside as the day of rest that God has commanded us to recognize. Yet, through the years, time has shown that we Christians have changed with the everchanging lifestyles of the world system, all because we had access to the "almighty" dollar, the one in whom we truly had our trust for if we trusted God, as we say we do, we would have stayed out of the shopping malls, restaurants, and other non-urgent places of business. Yet, because we had the one we trusted in, in our hands (be it plastic, paper, coin, or any other form of legal tender) we chose to demonstrate in whom we trusted and lusted rather than honoring this day of rest in obedience to God, whom we say we love.

Nehemiah, the Governor of Judah appointed by the Persian King Artaxerxes, exercised his legal authority to ban the selling of fish and other ware on the Lord's day when non-believers came to the gates of the city to sell to the children of God (Nehemiah 13:16-22). You may not be the Governor of your state but you are of your home and you are in the best position to cause a change right where it can take immediate hold if you will make a decision, right now, to reverence the Lord on the day you call your Lord's Day of Rest.

You can not call the day you attend Worship Services the Lord's Day of Rest when your actions cause some other Christian to have to work to attend to your non-emergency indulgences. While some may question the validity of using such ancient Scriptures for such a modern-day society, just remember: we will never walk in the spiritual anointing found in Scripture until we return to a Scriptural way of life. The best way to exemplify your love for God rather than money and bring your family's finances back under discipline is to govern your home's financial activities on the Lord's Day of Rest. If you can tackle that day, He will help you with your financial activities the rest of the week.

Doublemindedness. Solomon's sin of marrying outlandish woman who served other gods caused him to be doubleminded. Nehemiah reminded the Jews returning to Judah of this over 500 years later when they had fallen into the same sin. (Neh 13:26)

Covetousness. When you purpose to start giving to others' needs, out of every paycheck, if necessary, you will keep the spirit of covetousness away.

"I have coveted no man's silver, or gold, or apparel..." (Acts 20:33)
"He coveteth greedily all the day long: but the righteous giveth and and spareth not." (Prov 21:26)

Covetousness breeds a spirit of Envy, Greed, Materialism and Lust:

Envy--Harboring an inner resentment of another person who enjoys owning an asset you desire to possess.

Greed-- A self-centered desire to acquire more and more and more material possessions either out of insecurity or comparison.

Materialism-- Worshiping material possession which results in preoccupation with natural rather than spiritual blessings.

Lust-- A desire to get for self-gratification; a perversion of love which desires to give (people and ministry centered).

Evil Associations. King Jehoshaphat was extremely prosperous during his reign. He had riches and honor in abundance, yet because he joined with the wicked husband of Jezebel, King Ahab, and later with their son, King Ahaziah, who also did wickedly, God could not continue to let Jehoshaphat prosper (II Chron 18:1). When he joined himself with King Ahaziah to make merchant ships , the LORD sent a prophecy saying, *"Because thou hast joined thyself with Ahaziah, the LORD hath broken thy works."* and the ships were broken, that they were not able to go (II Chron 20:35-37). Jehoshaphat's prosperity was stifled because of these two unions with darkness.

That friendship that you have with that witchcraft worker; that member of freemasonry, eastern stardom, or any other fraternal or sororital order based on paganism and idolatry; liars, cheaters, adulterers, etc. is stifling your finances. I don't care if they are faithful workers in your church or a close blood relative; get that dead man off your back!

"CHRISTIANS AND THE CIRCULATION OF GOD'S DOLLAR WITHIN THE WORLD SYSTEM"

The president of a nationally known business which merchandizes personal and household products appeared on a nationally syndicated talk show on March 1, 1994. He announced that due to the openness of society he was coming out of the closet about his association with the church of Satan. He stated that a large portion of the profits from his consumer supported business goes to support the Satanic Church. When asked by the talk show host if stating this on national television would hurt his business, he replied, *"There aren't enough Christians in the United States to make a difference."*

IS HE CORRECT?

Pride. Lucifer's fall was based on his pride -- a desire to be worshiped. He looked at his appearance, abilities, and accomplishments and then boastfully puffed out the four "I Will's" (Isaiah 14:3). Pride will cause you to delve into worthless pleasures and to misappropriate God's funds, *"I have it; I'm going to spend it; I earned it; my kids aren't going to have it as hard as I had it" (your four I's).* Pride is based on vanity. The opposite of a vain person is a humble person. See Chapter 9 for wisdom from Solomon during his years of vanity.

Narrow-Minded, Self-Centeredness. In financial management, there's nothing worse than a person who will eat up his seed money. In ministry giving, tithes are seed money; offerings are seed money, so are vows and pledges.

Many people who are just getting started with their small businesses eat up their seed money. The money you use to start up your business is the seed money. This is not the time to give friends your "wares" free, reduced, or on a "pay when you can" basis. This is the time to seed back into the business. That is, after ministry seeds (tithe, offerings, vows, pledges) you must also seed back into the business. That is, this is not the time to buy a larger home, more expensive cars, more expensive clothes, and other self-indulgences. Have you ever heard of the term, "nouveau riche"? It's a person made newly rich. They are quite extravagant and lavish in spending their funds on items which make a display of their wealth. Learn to seed into the ministry, seed into the business, give, continue meeting your family's basic needs and then watch your business grow. (See my workbook, *Family Planner,* for a suggested format to follow in setting up and managing your business turn-over income.) The planting directions are right in the Bible:

*"So is the kingdom of God, as if a man should cast seed ($) into the ground (**the soil = ministry & business**); And should sleep, and rise night and day (**a time of waiting**), and the seed should*

*spring and grow up (**spiritually multiply**), he knoweth not how* ***(God did it!)***. *For the earth* ***(same ground)*** *bringeth forth fruit* ***(increase)*** *of herself ....But when the fruit is brought forth....the harvest* ***(prosperous yield)*** *is come." Mark 4:26-29* ***(bold**=my insertions)*

No Fear of God. You've seen the "No Fear" emblem on car windows, tee shirts, jackets and other clothing apparel. No fear of whom? Man? God? Both? It's dangerous to live through life without fearing God; nevertheless, we do it every day when we make decisions without first seeking direction from God. Financial wisdom and knowledge begin with first fearing the Lord (Prov 1:7, 9:10, 15:33). Yet, because we have no fear of God --

•We are snared by what we spend our money on. (Prov 14:27)

•We've lost our financial strength by placing our confidence in the dollar rather than in God. (Prov 14:26)

•We have financial treasures with troubled hearts. (Prov 15:16)

•We've lost our access to true riches. (Prov 22:4)

•We've stopped keeping the commandments of God; we've left the whole duty of man. (Ecclesiastes 12:13)

REPENTANCE FROM FINANCIAL SINS

Repentance involves an acknowledgement that you have sinned and a turning from that sin in your actions.

You and God. Some financial sins require only repentance to God but most require repentance to another individual too, because God has placed this person in position to receive from you on His behalf. This also keeps you accountable to someone, especially when an extenuating circumstance existed, causing you to fall into financial sin, rather than outright slothfulness or embezzlement.

You, God and a 3rd Person, the Offended Individual. Financial breaches between you and an offended person must be settled with repentance and restitution.

Restitution. All financial offenses against another individual require some form of restitution. That restituted amount is up to the individual owed: That person may extend the grace and mercy to --

    • cancel part of the debt (Luke 16:5-7)

    • cancel all of the debt (Matt 18:26-27)

or he may take the prerogative to

    • require all the debt to be paid in full (Matt 18:33-35)

    • require all the debt plus interest to be paid (Deu 23:20, Dan 6:24)

Forgiveness. If the offending individual is not you but the other party, God expects you to forgive them. Even if they don't honor any agreed upon restitution, you must forgive them to release yourself from acquiring a bitter spirit, shield yourself from retaining their sin, and keep yourself pure that God may forgive you when you sin,

"Whose soever sins ye remit, they are remitted unto them; and whose soever sins ye retain, they are retained." John 20:23

"For if ye forgive men their trespasses, your Heavenly Father will also forgive you: But if ye forgive not....neither will your Father forgive your trespasses." Matt 6:14-15

If you are the offending party, when repenting, if that person doesn't forgive you, you must still ask forgiveness that you might acquire a spiritual release from your sin.

CHAPTER 3

FINANCIAL VOWS AND PLEDGES

THE SERIOUSNESS OF A FINANCIAL VOW

We don't take vows seriously enough. We think of them as a heartfelt desire we'd like to fulfill if God supplies the extra money and if nothing else that pertains to self-desire comes up, first. A vow is not to be treated as a careless slip of the lips. Do you realize that the spiritual kick-back of an unfulfilled vow is so potent that it makes the destructive explosion of a stick of dynamite look like a balloon popping! An unfulfilled vow can not be written off, even by the person who received the vow from you on behalf of the LORD. This point is so grave in the area of unleashing evil spirits of financial consumption upon your hard-earned income that you need to take a few minutes, right now, to read all these Scriptures before continuing in this book:

- Lev 27:2,13
- Num 30
- Deu 23:21-23
- Job 22:27
- Psalm 15:4
- Psalm 50:14
- Psalm 66:13, 14
- Psalm 61:8
- Psalm 76:11
- Prov 20:25
- Eccles 5:4-6
- Acts 5:4
- Acts 18:18

There are additional Scriptures on vows that you will find listed in your concordance that state that the vow is always made "unto the Lord".

VITAL POINTS ABOUT A VOW
- A vow is a promise to God; a debt to God.
- God holds you to it.

• Because it is not made man to man, it can not be cancelled by man.

• When fulfilled, it is rewarded.

• When not fulfilled, although the Old Testament penalty of death is nullified by the cross, Satan still takes advantage of the legal ground we have given him to send an influx of tormenting evil spirits onto our finances till that loophole has been closed by fulfillment of the vow.

Unscriptural vows can be broken; sometimes women make unscriptural vows. Num 30:3-8

THE FINANCIAL COVENANT OF A VOW

A vow is a covenant between you and God. Strong's Concordance defines covenant as:

> **B⁵riyth: heb. (#1285)** -- *a compact, made by passing between pieces of flesh, in the sense of cutting.*

Here, we see a covenant is a bond in blood. It is a very sacred bond because it's made between man and God, and between God and man. Many people mistakenly consider that a covenant is the same thing as a modern-day contract. Yet, this is not true. People still make covenants today: those getting married, doctors (hypocratic oath), masons, witches making pacts with Satan (Prov 7:10,14; Jeremiah 44:25), etc. Both are binding agreements -- the covenant, made to God; the contract , made to man. Let's look at the most important aspects of a covenant that makes it uniquely a witness of the bond between you and God:

* A covenant establishes a Vow between you and God.

* This covenant is birthed out of mutual trust.

* This covenant is binding, regardless of circumstances.

COVENANT TESTS AND FAILURES

There are clear incidents in the Bible where

God tested covenants and men breached them. One such clear incident is that of the sweet wafer angel food, Manna, that God provided to feed the children of Israel in the wilderness. In that covenant God told Israel that He would deliver it daily, except the Sabbath, for He would deliver twice as much on the day prior to, that there would be no gathering on the Sabbath. Those who didn't heed to God's Manna Provision Covenant and gathered on the Sabbath saw that what they had gathered in disobedience had turned to worms.

Suppose you were to make a financial covenant with God: *"Heavenly Father, If you'll give me $100,000, I'll get out of this debt for sure; then I'll be able to bless your kingdom work. I'll pay my tithes, pay off my car, house, and bills and then seed the rest into the ministry. I'll start managing your money right, Father. Just wait and see, Lord."* Then, as a test, God sends you $1,000,000 instead of $100,000. Are you going to honor your covenant with Him? Are you going to pay your tithes, pay off all debt and then give the rest to bless His kingdom work?

Do you see why God does not abundantly bless all Christians with great excess in finances? He only chooses to pass large sums of money, that is intended to bless ministry work, through the hands of trust-worthy stewards; only they will see beyond the 10% and a little token love offering. If you can not be faithful with managing a little (income from your God-given job, skills and talent) your Heavenly Father can not entrust to your management the true riches of heaven (Luke 16:10).

Sometimes God will even initiate a covenant with you. It was just about four months from the day that I was penning the manuscript of this book that the LORD awakened me early in the darkness of the morning saying He would separate me out for a certain task and that, in turn, I had to vow to separate out. Just a few months prior I had read in a very spiritual book by a current author that the Lord had asked the same of her. Upon reading her testimony then, I thought, *"Surely God wouldn't require a covenant vow today, that's ancient."* But now here He was asking the same of me. I vowed to enter into this covenant and separated myself unto the LORD and as the consecration of the LORD was upon my head, eight days later during an early morning prayer, I saw the form of the Holy Spirit, outlined in "light" with swollen cheeks, blowing upon me as I continued praying; then He disappeared. The covenant sealed the spiritual mission the LORD had called me to and the word of spiritual prosperity that He had spoken the previous year. I entered into covenant that morning with the LORD, a covenant which I take very seriously. The covenants God makes with us are sealed with His promise, *"My covenant will I not break, nor alter the thing that is gone out of my lips"* *(Psalm 89:34).* We must be just that committed to Him when we open our mouths to make something as sacred as a covenant vow to Him.

Let's learn wisdom from Israel's breach of covenant with God while in the wilderness (Psalm 78:17-41):

• They continued to murmur and complain about the manna and other provisions God had made for them.

• God eventually gave them their lustful desire, meat.

• They eventually left their covenant relationship with God.

• Their stubbornness in the wilderness tempted God and limited Him.

In your time of continual financial lack, if you can not find a natural reason for this shortage, it is probably God who has placed you there, either for spiritual growth or chastisement. Just remember that He will not forsake you. Just learn to live on the supernatural provisions He makes for you, no matter how unglamorous they may be, and He will bring you out when what He has purposed in you has surfaced.

FINANCIAL PLEDGES

Financial pledges are made by the borrower to the lender to commit to repay a certain indebtedness under certain specified terms, for a certain period of time, until completion of payoff, with any adverse points and restitutions affixed and agreed upon by both parties. Pledges are executed by contracts (sometimes called promissory notes) between the two parties. Some examples of financial obligations that require pledges:

➤ Credit Cards   ➤Loans   ➤Car Notes
➤Mortgages   ➤College Loans   ➤Leases
➤Department Store Charge Cards

VITAL POINTS ABOUT A PLEDGE

• Made to a lender
• Made with same commitment as a vow; a promise to pay, *"I will pay...vows which my lips...uttered...*
when I was in trouble." Psalm 66:13-14
• Not paying = **SIN** (Ezekiel 18:5-17)

Father	Righteous Man	➤	Restores Pledge	Just, Godly Right, Life (vs 5-9)
Son	Sinful Man	➤	Doesn't Restore Pledge	Robber Abomination(vs 10-13)
Grand son	Righteous Man	➤	Restores Pledge	Just, Godly Right, Life (vs 14-17)

We see from the above analysis of what the Scriptures say, that each man does bear fruit of his own sins and each man's consequences occur as a result of his chosen actions. Sin was sin in the Old Testament; it was sin in the New Testament; and it's still sin today.

THE SERIOUSNESS OF FINANCIAL PLEDGES

A financial pledge is just as serious as a financial vow; it's just made to man instead of to God. The seriousness of the matter is that it must be honored as debt that must be paid. Its points of agreement are binding, as well. Let's look at the most important aspects of a contract that makes it different from the covenant of a vow:

- A contract establishes a pledge between you and man.
- All contracts are birthed out of distrust.
- All contracts can be mutually changed in terms, delayed, and even cancelled.

PLEDGING WITH WISDOM

The wisdom on making financial pledges is that you not strap yourself with more indebtedness than your budget can handle. When we don't honor pledges we've made, we find that the tormentors that Jesus spoke of in the parable in Matthew 18:34 are actually the enforcers of pledges we have made but brokened, *"And his lord was wroth, and delivered him to the tormentors, till he should pay all that was due unto him."* God wants us to avoid being victims of such torments; thus, He has also placed in His Word sound advice to consider before entering into a pledge:

If You Have To Borrow, Use Effective Borrowing Power. When the widowed wife of one of the prophets was harassed by creditors, Elisha gave her a method of borrowing that increased what little she had. She borrowed as many pots as she could from others to pour into them what little oil she had in the house. Her borrowing was lucrative. If God ever presents an opportunity to you that will place you in a position to borrow to stir up an increase that a little seed that you already have in your possession might multiply, then is the time to borrow.

Always Try To Cancel Out Debt With a Yield. In Luke 16: 5-7 we see a steward who called upon all those who owed his lord large sums of debt but he wrote off most of the debt (50% for one debtor, 20% for another). This steward was in the position to collect debt from pledges. Being judged by his lord as one who wasted goods, this steward turned that judgement around by gaining the favor of the debtors, reducing the actual balance on the amounts they owed his lord. Although this passage is about a person who represents the institution who makes the loan, there is sound advice here for the one who borrows money, too. Always put yourself in a position that you will gain FAVOR in the eyes of your lender so when your finances fail, they will have mercy on you, granting terms that only God can divinely impart.

Use Communication Doorways. How often we forget that misunderstandings occur between husband and wife, sibling and sibling, boss and employee, etc. due to lack of communication. Who knows whether they would have turned off your phone, if you'd only told them about the emergency trip to another state to see your dying sister? Maybe they would have re-adjusted your payment on a particular bill instead of summoning a judgement against you, if they'd only known about your job lay off due to company closure....etc.

Hebrews 13:16 tells us to communicate, *"...but*

to do good and to communicate forget not: for with such sacrifices God is well pleased."

In Luke 24:15, we see Simon and Cleopas reasoning together through verbal communication, *"...while they communed together and reasoned, Jesus himself drew near, and went with them."*

We are advised in Luke 16:9 to be friendly with our lender that when we have nothing to pay, we will gain favor through the existing rapport we've already established, *"Make to yourselves friends of the mammon of unrighteousness: that when ye fail, they may receive you into everlasting habitation."*

The bottom line is simply to speak up when you foresee a problem, preferably before the payment is due. You can telephone, write or visit but a visit is more personable because of eye-to-eye contact; thus, your apparel is also important. In any event, we are looking to open communication doorways and keep them opened long after your pledge has been satisfied. Who knows, they might just come to you for a favor in the future and because of the excellent rapport you have with them today, they have nothing but laudatory imprints in their memory and in their files on you!

CHAPTER 4

FINANCIAL CURSES

THE INVISIBILITY OF A CURSE

*"...be filled with...all wisdom and spiritual understanding... of the **invisible God**... For by Him were all things created .....visible and **invisible** ......"* (Colossians 1: 9-16)

When you find money draining from your hands in many financial situations you could be caught up in an "invisible hole" resulting from a curse on your money. Such curses usually exist behind many money consuming transactions such as car repairs, car purchases, fast cash loans, and door-to-door sales to name a few. Such evil spiritual entrappings are just financial vacuums that will suck every ounce of air out of your budget, your time with the Lord, your family life, and even your marriage.

REASONS FOR FINANCIAL CURSES

- Not paying tithes and offerings (Mal 3:8-9)
- Generational sin
- Witchcraft curses
- Trusting the arm of man, not God (Jer 17:5)

SIGNIFICANT POINTS ABOUT CURSES

- A curse is a spiritual problem which can not be remedied by natural means.
- Where sin is, the curse remains.
- The power of a curse is demonic.
- Yes, Christ has redeemed us from the curse but the **redemption must be appropriated.**

THE CURSE OF THE LAW vs GRACE & MERCY

It's hard to believe, isn't it, that I would claim

that curses still apply to Christians as well as to non-believers. But, before you put this book down, bear with me for a moment while I explain what the Scriptures mean by appropriating the redemptive blood of Jesus. Below is a depiction of two Christians: one under the umbrella of Jesus' blood covering of grace (safe from curses); the other, one who walked out from under the covering due to sin but who is, now, on his way back (repentance) to reclaim covering (grace) once realizing he is now getting wet in the rain (the curse of the law).

The wandering Christian above doesn't realize generational sins still exist; he was just covered when he was under Jesus' umbrella of grace. Only after he has stepped out from under the protection of the blood, by committing personal sin, does he realize that the spoken witchcraft curses and the generational sins which were in operation against his unsaved siblings were now trying to bind him. (Committing personal sin wedges a "hole" that gives legal ground for generational sins and witchcraft curses to actively oppress you.)

What causes you to step out from under the grace covering of Jesus's blood? SIN.

Now taking a few more moments to re-examine the above illustration, answer these questions:

1. Could you also see yourself, at times, stepping out from under Jesus's blood covering of "Grace"?

2. Are you then spiritually uncovered and back in a place where, if Satan attacks you, you are vulnerable ?

3. Then, out from under Jesus' covering because of personal sin, could demonic activity tempt you by bringing other sins back to you which have been strongholds in your family's bloodline?

4. While you're out from under Jesus' blood covering of grace, would it be easier to get you to sin by presenting something that has already been proven a weakness in the past in your family line or in some sin you committed before salvation?

5. Now that you see this pattern, vividly, if you're out from under Jesus' blood covering, right now, when are you going to repent, get that hole covered, get out of those wet clothes and run back under the covering of Jesus' umbrella of grace? ....NOW!!!

Notice also the sins showering down in the above illustration. Could any of these sins, permitted to stay around, tamper with your financial discipline? Let's see.....

Lust, Greed, Covetousness after Clothing?
➔ YES

Lust, Greed, Covetousness after Material Items?
➥ YES
Drinking Alcohol?
➥ YES
Drug Addiction?
➥ YES
Adulterous Relations, Fornication?
➥ YES
Homosexuality?
➥ YES
Abortion?
➥ YES
Kleptomania, Embezzlement?
➥ YES
Occult Associations (paraphernalia, organizations, etc.)
➥ YES
Accomplice to Sins of Others
➥ YES
Gluttony
➥ YES, etc.

Yes, all of the above sins, and others, eat away at your finances. They need the money you are supposed to be using to support your family, pay tithes and offerings, seed into ministry work and help the poor to pull you away, gradually, and continually resupply your fleshly appetite. Your flesh first indulges, monetarily, then demons of consumption come along to help you kill off the rest of your finances.

GENERATIONAL CURSES

The LORD allowed me to come in contact with a large church-going family which consisted of twelve children. This family unknowingly lived under witchcraft curses much of their lives which caused major hindrances in finances, marriage relations, child bearing, and even early death in first-borns. The curses were pronounced on the father which caused a ripple effect in the children's lives in varying degrees depending on their individual relationships with God as they matured. Generational curses eventually evolved out of these originally pronounced word curses. We're just going to look at their financial generational curses in this book.

As the siblings matured into young adults, some became born-again, Holy Spirit-filled Christians; some continued as church-goers, and some did not. With similar educational backgrounds, those settling far away from home fared better financially than those near their hometownship, regardless of their relationship with God. A few of these siblings never married. The majority of those who married experienced major financial incidents in their marriages and most first time marriages failed. Three of those marriages were childless. While many of the other marriages experienced very premature deaths in the first-born child from these unions. Some tithing Christian siblings lived better under the curse than some other tithing Christian siblings. Certain ones were closer to the LORD than others in their walk, but this still did not provide an absolute shield from the curses, for some who were more dedicated than others to the LORD (not to church projects, but to the LORD) fared less well off financially because of marriages to others who had varying degrees of generational curses pulling at them that brought other curses into the marriage by the union of offsprings from two different families. (Do you see how combinations play here, too?) I won't go any deeper into this web, for a finance book isn't the place. I just want to present to you a complete enough picture of a real-to-life family experiencing real curses that you might see that you are not immune to the effects of curses seeping into your finances.

WITCHCRAFT CURSES

When situations are brought on by spoken witchcraft curses upon your finances, depending upon your response, you could open the door to the controlling presence of satanic evil spirits. If such doors are opened, generational curses are set in motion which will have varying degrees of effects on the offsprings of the one receiving the witchcraft curse, depending on their individual walks with the LORD.

The LORD arranged it that I would meet such a man. This man confessed to me that he had a "money demon". I noticed that whenever it was time for him to receive money (paycheck or other income) he'd become very anxious, irritable and driven. This man had lost a large amount of property and real estate, received several court judgments against him, and had experienced other major financial failures. I later learned that this man had been the victim of a major witchcraft scheme and an evil spirit of financial consumption had been sent upon him by a covetous family of witches who had master-minded this scheme. Because of this man's doublemindedness -- an active church-goer, deacon and trustee of the church, Mason, and past practitioner of witchcraft himself who had not broken ties with his affiliates -- the witchcraft curses activated and thrived. This man was the father of the siblings experiencing generational curses in the previous paragraph.

THE LESSONS LEARNED FROM
THIS STORY

Here are the significant points you need to retain from the previous true story:

•**Witchcraft curses on your finances are**

territorial. That's why some individuals in an immediate family who live within the zone of the satanist performing such incantations against that family will experience more financial failures than the individual with the same incantation upon him but living in another State, even when the one living further away is living a lifestyle that is not as close to God as the one who lives within the zone of the witch. I've experienced this type of control, many times, with attacks on my car when I was commuting a long distance to work for a long period of time. A particular witch would send spirits to make my car overheat. The LORD showed me how to cast out the demons but I had to make the three hour drives on faith for the car continued to register "overheating". Each time, as I drove out of the territorial control zone, the needle erected. The first time this occurred I praised the LORD for healing my car; yet, on the way back that evening as I approached their territorial zone, the needle on my temperature gauge became depressed again; yet the car never actually overheated as I drove on faith for several months. I experienced this same kind of control when another witch made my car slip sideways into the side lane of traffic, for several days, yet with no harm. The LORD's protection kept me and my purse that I didn't have to spend His money on car repairs or worse.

　　•**Witchcraft curses can only achieve their appointed end when you are in sin.** Sin gives Satan legal access to conquer surrendered ground; captivity always follows surrender. Even when not in sin, these curses can temporarily hinder you (Isaiah 17:10-11).

"For the rod of the wicked shall not rest upon the righteous; lest the righteous put forth their hands unto iniquity." (Psalm 25:3)

　　•**Although you may not be sinning, evil associations may make you vulnerable to hindrance.**

See "What Causes Us To Commit Financial Sins",
Chapter 2.

> •**This could just be on-hands training for
you.** Sometimes when you can't pin a particular personal sin or an association to your having to experience the oppression of a curse, God may be allowing it
for on-hand experience, just to prepare you for something else ahead.

> •**Prosperity comes when oppression leaves.**

*"Many of them also which used curious arts brought their
books together, and burned them before all men: and they counted
the price of them, and found it fifty thousand pieces of silver. So
mightily grew the Word of God and prevailed."* (Acts 19:19-20)

TOUCH NOT THE ACCURSED THING

If you find yourself having to deal with such
sorcery don't be afraid; God says to fear no man. Find
your comfort and assurance in the Word of God as you
follow His lead in breaking loose from such control.
Start with studying these Scriptures:

Exodus 22:18	Leviticus 19:31	Leviticus 20:6,27
Deut 18:10-12	Job 30:3-8	Isaiah 54:14-17
Micah 5:8-13	Nahum 3:4-7	Zech 3:2-5
Malachi 3:5	Matthew 4:10	Matthew 16:23
Mk 16:17-18	Luke 10:17-19	John 8:44
Acts 10:38	Romans 16:20	I Cor 15:55-57
II Cor 10:4-6	Hebrew 2:14	James 4:7
I John 3:8	Isaiah 47:8-15	Isaiah 55:11

Then, Praise God!

Rev 5:12-13	Rev 7:12	Rev 12:11
Rev 4:8, 11	Rev 11:15, 17	Rev 19:4-7a

Additionally, if you don't want a spoken word
curse to alight and take effect when spoken against
you, you can not be using God's money to finance
your curiosity, delving into the unknown, and fanciful.
All of the following demon empowered activities or

paraphernalia will hinder your financial flow:
- Astrology
- Free Masonry
- Lottery (Deu 18:10)
- Wearing of Occult Symbols
- Ancient Artifacts
- Hand Writing Analysis
- Lucky Charms

- Mind Control Activities: *Hypnosis* *Martial Arts* *Levitation* *Meditation* *Yoga* *Mind Reading* *Psychics*

- Images of Idolatry *(This includes dolls and puppets. Witchcraft workers use these otherwise harmless items tremendously today.)*

THE IMPACT OF CURSES ON FINANCIAL CHANGES AND NEW BEGINNINGS

A job change, promotion, retirement and many other "entering and exiting" financial changes you can think of are times when anyone speaking a word curse over your finances can hinder your good start (especially when your new start occurs at the crest of a natural change, i.e. Seasons and time changes). Satan uses these times to bind your financial flow so that it will not reach the apex of what it should be. Demons can place a myriad of situational incidents into play here. When my son, the firstborn grandchild completed high school, with honors, we had a financial failure which was short-lived (6 weeks) and immediately went into a spiral of financial prosperity. I did not know then that the failure, stemming from a car totaling accident with injuries, was engineered by witchcraft, but God knew. The LORD also knew I had to do something to turn it around. I didn't understand, at that time, why He told me to give $1,000 to the church's building fund when I had already given

$1,000 some time prior, when I had no automobile to drive, and college expenses were starting up the next month. However, I obeyed Him and by the end of the week, two beautiful cars paid for in cash!

The Lord Jesus Christ wants you to go through financial changes to elevate you, not depress you. Change is a time to reap blessings in your financial flow. You need to grasp this revelation and run with it. See also "Entering and Exiting Financial Windows", Chapter 16.

The purpose of witchcraft curses on your finances is to bring you into financial bondage. God will not make new money for you when you come out of a financial curse. He releases captured money held in bondage. His restoration could flow from held back job promotions, insurance settlements, investment yields, inheritances, business sales, misappropriated funds, etc. God is in the business of restoring but it is our business to get in position, spiritually, to receive His deliverance and restoration.

DEMONS OF CURSES

As was mentioned earlier, the power of a curse is demonic. Even a witch is just a helpless old jealous wind-bag without the leading of her/his familiar spirit, demon spirit guide, counselor, or whatever you want to call it. She/he is just an instrument that the evil spirits use to connect with other human beings in a wrong way while at the same time reaching further back into the spiritual realm to connect with ruling spirits of darkness and spiritual wickedness in high places as they reach further back to Satan, ole' Lucifer, himself, in disguise.

If you have problems with financial discipline it may not be due to a curse of any type or it may. Take note, if you are experiencing a continual pulling, repetitive hindrances or failures for unknown reasons especially when you've done all you can in extra borrowing and the taking on of additional jobs, you are probably being oppressed by a spirit of consumption. This spirit can be released upon you due to a generational curse, a spoken word curse, or another one I haven't even mentioned yet, a personal curse you've brought on yourself due to sin you've chosen to commit out of your own fleshly will.

Consumption spirits can lead you into much consumer debt, especially with the easy acquisition of credit cards. Consumption spirits come in colonies: spirits of covetousness, lust, greed, etc. Indulging in fleshly sins invite such money-using demons to suggest spending habits, which eventually place a strongman's stronghold on your finances.

Spirits of monetary consumption can also drain you in many other ways: unresolved automobile problems, misappropriated funds, and unresolved sickness to name a few. Sickness, in particular, for while you can not be diagnosed, you must continue to pay for the testing, hospitalization, second and third opinions, new procedures, etc.

BREAKING THE POWER OF CURSES
OFF YOUR FINANCES

This is not a cut and dried area either. You need to go to Father God and ask Him specifics when you know you have to deal with this type of closure. Even if you think, "It might be but it might not be". Wouldn't it be a blessing to break a curse when it wasn't necessary rather than to go on ignoring that one exists when in actuality it does and you continue to bleed, needlessly?

Breaking the power of curses is Scriptural and necessary for, as mentioned earlier, a curse can't be

remedied by natural means. A spiritual problem must be dealt with spiritually; thus, if your finances are being hindered by a generational, witchcraft or self-committed sin curse, you need to do the following:
• Repent of any sins (specifically)
• Forgive others (specifically)

Then, in the name of "JESUS CHRIST":
• Break generational curses (Be specific; break them off your kids, too.)
• Break personal sin curses
• Break spoken word curses
• Denounce all association with Satan (Occult areas mentioned above, etc., and separate out from those involved in such in your family, too, if they don't first respond to evangelism.)
• Cleanse your home of such articles and activities of association. (Read Part V, Chapters 21-22, thoroughly, in the book *Raising Responsible Children In a Single-Parent Home.* Apply it; then anoint your family and home.)

The Christian children and offsprings birthed from the family addressed earlier eventually experienced deliverance from the financial bondages/hindrances resulting from the curses spoken on the forefather and the ensuing generational curses his actions brought forth upon them. They became prosperous, many marriages were restored, and they were blessed to enjoy the fruit of their labor. (The mother, whom I have not mentioned thus far, was even given an anointed healing ministry from the LORD for her deliverance was from schizophrenic spirits sent upon her by this very same major witchcraft scheme.)
Some releases from spiritual strongholds on your finances cannot be released just by following the

"breaking" procedures addressed above, alone. Sometimes other spiritual releases beyond your control must occur. In this particular family, when the father died, the releases came. Even the one Christian sibling who was seen by the other Christian siblings as being very prosperous even during this bondage period confided in me that their prosperity resulted from their pro actively pressing forward even in financial matters which seemed unfruitful; They would not take "no" for an answer. They still felt the hindrances on every financial dealing they were involved in. Yet, they continued to press through in every dealing and responded to every opportunity God gave them to sacrificially give which they felt attributed to their mastering over the oppression of this consumption spirit that seem to be ever present but never victorious.

I shared just the financial part of this hybrid example of family curses with you to show how relying on divine intervention, when all human effort is exhausted, will many times be the only way of loosening the bound and releasing the captives. Destroying curses off your family finances isn't a pretty 1, 2, 3, procedural step. Everybody's stronghold is different. Just start to do the suggestions above and GOD will reveal any unique areas you will have to deal with that aren't addressed here.

THE SPIRITUAL GIFT OF
DISCERNING OF SPIRITS

God has planted gifts in the body as he pleases (I Cor 12:18). It seriously grieves me to see how the church body has gone without the gift of "discerning of spirits" today and how those with this gift are made to feel as if they are mentally unstable and imbalanced even by those filled with the Holy Spirit. I encourage you, if you have this gift, don't be discouraged. God has graciously endowed you with something precious. Don't look on the faces of the unbelieving; don't despise God's gift because others don't understand it. Even when leadership comes against you or pushes you aside when God is trying to speak to them through you because He knows He has given you this special gift, don't become discouraged. Remember, even when Saul sought to destroy David, David still respected him and said, *"I will not touch God's anointed."* Those who are truly God's called will eventually see what God shows you as spiritual truth. God will eventually disclose your unequivocal stand for Him.

I preface this section with this statement because most of what I share with you here is through my experiences from the operation of this spiritual gift that God chose to give me for ministry to others in spiritual bondages. Many people don't realize that many of their financial problems are based on a spiritual problem that you can not see with the natural eye; thus, many of our financial problems are just coated over with more debt.

When I was planning personal budgets through church ministry, it was through this gift that God made me aware of specific spiritual sources for some financial problems persons were experiencing. It is also through this gift that the LORD shows me areas of ministry to people who are afflicted by workers of witchcraft. I hope you are receiving some revelation knowledge here, too, as the LORD guides me in penning this, what I hope, is edifying information.

The characteristics of one having the Holy Spirit's gift of discernment of spirits include, being able to discern --
  • the presence of evil spirits.
  • the condition of human spirits, especially

when their underlying nature is quite different from that projected at a given time.

•approaching danger.

•the presence of angelic spirits (in visionary and human form).

•glimpses of hidden conditions in the spirit realm surrounding ulterior motives intentionally covered up in the natural realm.

Such discernments can not be readily made, at call, by the person with the gift. That person is only provided periodic discernment by the Holy Spirit as God so leads and deems necessary.

TITHES AND OFFERINGS

As this subject is addressed thoroughly in many books and publications on the market today, discussions on tithes and offerings is disbursed throughout this book. I will emphasize four points here, though, because they are not addressed in many books on the market :

1. The tithe that God requires could be either 10%, if paid as a first fruit or 30% if redeemed (cashed in, reclaimed by you, wrongfully). This 30% amount equals the original amount God commanded plus a 20% penalty. (Lev 22:14, 27:31, fifth part =20%)

2. Tithes and offerings are not the only form of spiritual multiplication mentioned in the Old Testament. The hundredfold blessing was also reaped in the Old Testament. Therefore, it was possible to also reap 30/60-fold blessings (which are less than 100-fold) during Old and New Testament times. (Isaac's 100-fold blessing, Gen 26:12, was based on what he sowed.)

3. The Bible only recognizes 3 basic forms of ministry giving: Tithes, Offerings and Vows/Pledges. When giving church offerings, don't be concerned if

you can never arrive at the point where you are able to contribute to every item listed on the tithing envelope. Your finances will not be cursed because you aren't giving to every area listed.   The tithes are clearly shown on the envelope. All other areas are various types of offerings. Even Vows and Pledges listed are still offerings; yet, they should be listed separately because they represent personal commitments which must be tracked for accountability.

4. As the Church continues to address a 10% tithe plus free will offerings, the world system has gone on from 20% to 28% and higher in its assessments on our income:

Scripturally -- Gen 47:24-26; I Sam 8:11-17; Matt 17:24-27, 22:21.

Currently -- tax bracket rates, restaurant tips, gasoline sales taxes, etc.

It leaves one to wonder why a Christian would complain about a 10% tithe, grumble about an offering or debate about the legitimacy of one versus the other for a modern day Christian when the modern day world system assesses us increasingly higher rates to which we have no complaint.

TRUSTING THE ARM OF MAN, NOT GOD

The term "the arm of man" means, the strength, shoulder or power of the world system. The strength of the world system is what makes it operate. Money makes the world system operate. What are some of the many faces of money in our world system? Credit Cards, Department Charge Accounts, Consumer Loans, etc. These items represent non-liquidated money that seems to spend easier because you can't really see it. However, in the end, real money must be tendered at some point and at a high interest rate.

If you are constantly buying items using credit

cards and department charge accounts because you don't have the money, and when the bill arrives you still don't have the money to pay them off, you are trusting in the arm of man. If you steadily find yourself borrowing money to make ends meet, or to repetitively consolidate old debt, you are trusting in the arm of man. If when you look at your monthly budget plan you find a list of charge cards and loans, you are trusting in the arm of man. You have cursed yourself with a curse; your heart has departed from God as your source.

"Thus saith the LORD; Cursed be the man that trusteth in man, and maketh flesh his arm, and whose heart departeth from the LORD." (Jeremiah 17:5)

Just before my spiritual prosperity came and I was approaching the end of the wilderness stage (after having given God all I had 2 years prior -- job, home, material possessions, securities, retirement, etc.) the LORD told me to trust Him totally. I thought I had trusted Him; after all, I was now assisting the music director at church and assisting the secretary and all the money went toward paying my rent, utilities, and gas, after tithes and offerings. And that money was from Him. It was certainly holy money. But then the LORD clearly said to stop even that work and trust Him. So, I did. Three weeks later, the end of the month, my rent, utilities, etc. were due. One day before the end of the month, I received three checks and $50 cash and the very last day I received another check for $99.00. I had $348 in hand and I only needed $277 to meet my obligations.

"Therefore, take no thought, saying, What shall we eat? or, What shall we drink? or, Wherewithal shall we be clothed? .....for your Heavenly Father knoweth that ye have need of all these things. But seek ye first the kingdom of God....and all these things shall be added unto you." (Matthew 6:31-33)

CHAPTER 5

FINANCIAL IGNORANCE

SIGNS OF FINANCIAL IGNORANCE

• Not giving good quality to the poor (Deu 24:19-21)
• Giving beyond what you have (II Cor 8:12-15)
• Living on maximum of your income
• Not prioritizing (Your tithes - spiritual covering - and
    mortgage/rent - natural covering - are always
    first and second priority, respectively.)
• Indulgence in "Abundance of Idleness"

All of the above points are self-explanatory; yet, we tend to take the area of indulging in idleness a little too lightly.

ABUNDANCE OF IDLENESS

Many people fail to see the significance of the sin pattern of Sodom and Gomorrah that eventually led God to wipe them off the face of the earth! It's significant to this book because without money they would not have been able to indulge in these vain idlenesses You could call these sins "SEED SINS".

God says, *"I'll plant a seed, let it multiply and it will produce good fruit."* Satan says, *"I'll plant a seed-sin, let it multiply and it will produce a sin of the worst kind."* It was seed-sin, not good seed, which when multiplied led to Sodom and Gomorrah openly accepting the product-sin of homosexuality as an alternative lifestyle.

You won't find these seed-sins even mentioned in the story of Sodom and Gomorrah in Genesis 18-19. Instead God waits until Ezekiel 16:49-50 before He reveals these little foxes as He says:

All of these seed-sins are frequently overlooked by the church as being spiritually harmful because of their wide-spread acceptance. Yet, the most tremendously abused one in the church is the seed-sin of idleness. Idleness is embellished by the multitude of past-times and entertainment we engage in -- TV, movies, sporting events, social clubs, concerts and theatrical plays; self-enrichment pursuits such as seminars and conferences, ever learning and never able to come to the knowledge of the truth.

Our American society is currently indulging in the same seed-sins as those two Old Testament cities did. Unshamefacedly, our American Christian Churches are currently wilfully indulging in these same seed-sins. These seed-sins have become like little foxes which spoil the vine as the church points its finger at the product sin while our indulgence in the seed-sins goes unnoticed. There are many spend-thrift areas of indulgence that are never preached from the pulpit because they are practiced in the pulpit, too. Just what are these spend-thrift vanities that we over-extend an excessive amount of God's funds on? They are revenue consuming businesses and activities which thrive only during a period of "Abundance of Idleness" :

• Arts n' Crafts Shops	• Hair Art vs Hair Dos
• Body Tanning Salons	• Novelty Shops
• Body Building	• Pet Hospitals
• Banquet/Buffet Dining	• Pet Hair Styling
• 24 Hr Department Stores	• Pet Cemeteries
• 24 Hr Grocery Stores	• Pet Clinics

- Skin Tatoo Shops
- Social Clubs
- Frivolous Furniture
    -- Gossip Bench
- Pet Boarding/Hotels
- Pedicures/Manicures
- TVs/Movies/VCR's
- Toys Focusing on Material Gain, Competition, Human Power and Magic
- Increase In Body Perfumes
    --Book Stores
    --Pets
    --Institutions of Higher Learning

- Increase In Security Items
    --Security Systems
    --Specialty Insurances
    --Specialty Physicians
    --Specialty Phones, etc.

- Increase In Reveling, Rioting, Partying, Socio-Behavioral Activities & Criminal Acts

- Room Additions
    --Florida Rooms
    --Recreation Rooms
    --Garages

(Have you ever considered adding an Elisha Room? II Kings 4: 9-10)

Do you know where this list came from? The Holy Spirit prompted me to just skim through the yellow pages of a small town's telephone book. A small town, not a large metropolitan city. So, it's safe to assume that this list could even quadruple in size when considering the financially fueled idlenesses a large city has to offer.

We are trying to raise Christian families today in the middle of a society frocked with the seed-sins that fostered the pathway for homosexuality as an acceptable lifestyle even in ancient history. Don't help history to repeat itself. Do the little you can do by not falling into the danger of the seed-sins yourself. Gravitate to planting good seeds with God's money, letting those seeds multiply and produce good fruit for a healthy, God-centered society.

CHAPTER 6

FINANCIAL COVERINGS

THE BIBLICAL STRUCTURE OF COVERINGS

In II Corinthians 11:1 Paul admonishes the Christians of Corinth to, *"Be ye followers of me, even as I also am of Christ."* Here we see the concept of followers following leaders and, then, leaders being linked to Christ. He delineates the breakdown of the pattern of leader-follower even further in verse 3, *"...the head of every man is Christ: and the head of the woman is the man: and the head of Christ is God."*

This pattern provides a continual covering for the woman and for children, through the leadership of the male. This may not seem to represent the modern day pattern for every home doesn't have a male covering; yet, God has ordained that, spiritually, there will be a male covering for every family unit. The physical manifestation of this covering is seen through the male's responsibility to provide, financially, for the family. This is also enforced by court systems and social service agencies as men are usually the ones sought after to provide for the offsprings of a broken home and, in cases where the wife was a homemaker, the male is summoned to provide alimony for the woman who depended upon him to provide for her, financially, during the marriage's existing years.

Today, everyone is not under the proper financial coverings. Satan knows that the basis for proper financial coverings is founded on the Word of God and he will waste no time in holding up your life to the light of God's Word to see how you measure up. In short, if you are a female, you must be under the proper covering of a male: either your dad, granddad, husband, uncle, nephew, elder cousin, or pastor. A boyfriend is not a proper covering. Study how the Bible lays out this order in the illustration below.

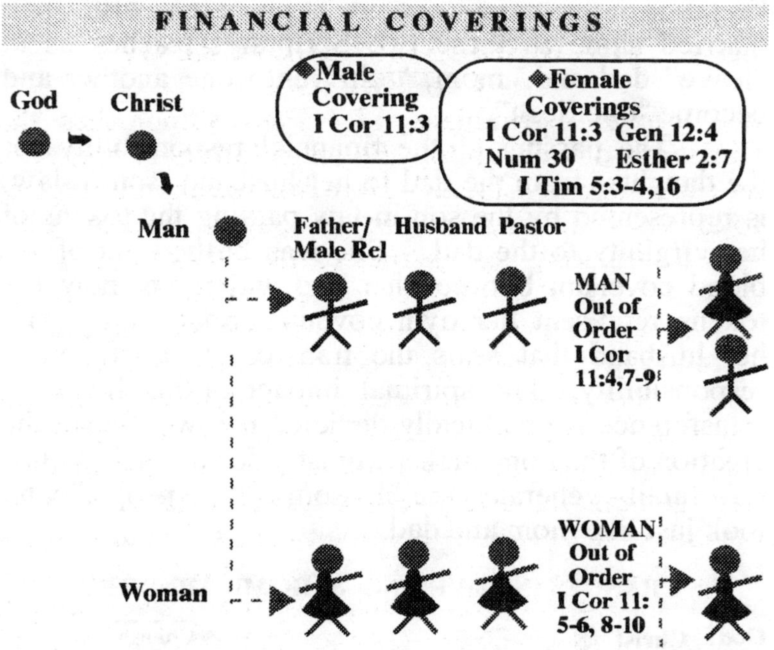

Scripturally, the man out of order in this illustration would be one whose marriage is dominated by his mother or another matriarch who perhaps raised him or he would be one who is henpecked by his wife. The woman out of order would be one who rejects a proper male covering or who henpecks, dominates, or manipulates her husband.

"And I find more bitter than death the woman, whose heart is snares and nets, and her hands as bands: whoso pleaseth God shall escape from her." Eccles 7:26

"And in that day seven women shall take hold of one man, saying, We will eat our own bread, and wear our own apparel: only

Additionally, Ephesians 5:31 and Genesis 2:24 make one consider the new wave, today, of women keeping their maiden name hyphenated with their married name as these two Scriptures teaches us to "leave" dad and mom, "join" unto one another and become "one flesh".

The passing of the financial responsibility for the daughter from the dad to her husband (son-in-law) is represented by the son-in-law passing the tokens of her virginity to the dad.   She was birthed out of the blood covenant between her dad and mom; now her tokens represent her own covenant relationship with her husband that seals the transfer of the financial responsibility. The spiritual impact of this financial transference is graphically depicted below. Notice the creation of the homemaker ministry for the wife as this new family generates and blossoms "little people" who look just like mom and dad.

CHANGES IN COVERING & HOME MINISTRY

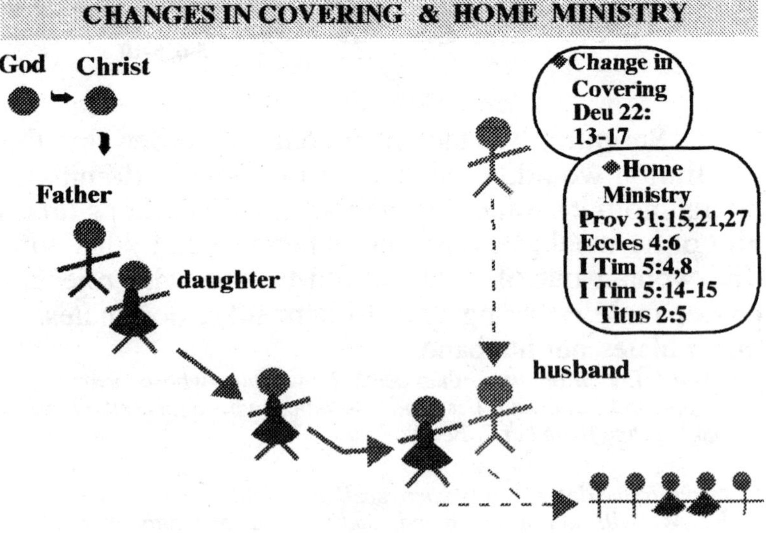

Because our society offers so much material-ism, we often subordinate the very necessary ministry of the home to the need to get ahead socially. The home ministry is very much needed today for the survival of the Christian family. In the Scriptures under Home Ministry in the illustration above, reference is made each time to the wife being the manager of the household and the one who guides and keeps the home. The message of Eccles 4:6, speaks very poignantly to the vexation that has occurred in many of today's two-parent working homes,

> *"Better is a handful **(husband's pay)** with quietness, than both the hands full (**both working**) with travail and vexation of spirit." **(bold**=my insertions)*

The two-parent income home has afforded the family an opportunity to raise it's materialistic stand-ard of living, at a sacrifice. (Sometimes barren-ness is due to disobedience. Psalm 128:3) God sacrificed His best for us, His son Jesus Christ our Savior and Lord. Our best sacrifice in return should center around our children, the sacrifice of things that we might redirect our focus to coming under the financial covering that God has already set in place for our financial success; with a little spiritual help from the LORD, we can work our way back to being "one flesh", financially.

THE FEMALE SINGLE PARENT

God honors and blesses female leadership -- in the church (under a male covering) and in the home (yet under a male covering). One example, financially, is when the Lord sent the widowed wife of one of the prophets, now a single parent with two sons, to Elisha for wisdom on multiplying her resources to pay her creditors (I Kings 4:1-7). Everywhere in Scripture where God has divinely ordained a woman to hold the highest position of leadership, it was God's "permissive" rather than His "perfect" will, at a period in time when appropriate male leadership was not available. Deborah, the only female judge, answered the call of God to lead when Barak said unto her, *"If thou wilt go with me, then I will go: but if thou wilt not go with me, then I will not go' (Judges 4:6-9).* After Deborah's very successful leadership, God reverted back to His "perfect" will of male leadership at the highest position of authority and as history unrolled only permissively allowed change, for a period of time, when godly male leadership had again waned (Isaiah 3:1-14). Thusly, female leadership in the home, in church, in businesses, etc. must be linked to a male covering to be blessed by God and receive His spiritual and natural protection.

SPIRITUAL PROTECTION

Even beyond the natural financial coverings that God has set in place, He has promised us spiritual protection at times when we may not be aware of a need for covering. Psalm 91 tells us that when we abide under the shadow of the Almighty He'll protect us from four seemingly insignificant, yet very important, occurrences. Yet, I truly believe that this spiritual protection is for those who follow God's above order of financial coverings. Draw close attention to verses 5-6:

Because we trust in His covering, we will not be afraid of the --

Occurrence	Type of Attack	When? Jewish Clock
1. Arrow	A Direct Assault (financial conflicts, harrassing phone calls)	Day (6am-12noon)

2. Destruction   A Direct Hit   Noonday (12noon-6pm)
                  (financial failures, crashes
                  forefeiture, foreclosure)

3. Terror   Unexpected,   Night (6pm-12midnite)
                  Unseen Tragedy
                  (burglary, intrusion, tragedy)

4. Pestilence   Oppression   Darkness (12midnite-6am)
                  (nightmares, insomnia
                  restlessness, walking spirits)

You may have never noticed that this short passage from Psalm 91 deals with covering, in a spiritual way. Now knowing that God's divine plan for your finances includes a natural commitment that must be executed by you, start today to follow what you can do, naturally, to bring your family in line with God's structure that you may invoke His spiritual covering as well.

CHAPTER 7

ASSOCIATION WITH PROSPEROUS PEOPLE

You can tell a prosperous person. He doesn't have to be rich; he can just attempt to do something and it flourishes; and those associating with him will flourish, too:

God to Abram

"And I will bless them that bless thee, and curse him that curseth thee: and in thee shall all families of the earth be blessed." Gen 12:3

Laban to Jacob

"For it was little which thou hadst before I came, and it is now increased unto a multitude; and the LORD hath blessed thee since my coming..." Gen 30:30

God to Joseph

" And the LORD was with Joseph, and he was a prosperous man...the LORD made all that he did to prosper in his hand ...the LORD blessed the Egyptian's house for Joseph's sake; and the blessing of the LORD was upon all that he had in the house, and in the field." Gen 39:2-6

The seven statutes sealing the covenant that God would make with a prosperous man are built around what God knows he will do for others. They are right in Genesis 12:2-3 as the LORD speaks to Abram (Abraham):

<u>God's Word To Abram</u>	<u>A Blessing For</u>
1. I will make of thee a great nation ⟹	his offsprings
2. I will bless thee ⟹	his prosperity
3. I will make thy name great ⟹	his prosperity
4. Thou shalt be a blessing ⟹	others
5. I will bless them that bless thee ⟹	others
6. You will bless all families ⟹	others

Then There Is The Flip Side:
7. I will curse them that curse thee ➠ a curse to others

You see, prosperity isn't all about money and material possessions, alone. It's about accountability, reliability, availability, stewardship and selflessness.

CHAPTER 8

LEARNING TO GIVE

This chapter addresses Giving as it relates to the work of God's ministry within and outside the church. Beyond the tithe, which is a sacred portion God has set aside to support the pastor, the poor and persons working in levitical positions within the church, there is a giving portion which consists of free will offerings, vows and pledges in monetary resources; of time and skills in human resources; and of personal possessions in material resources. Vows and Pledges are discussed in Chapter 3.

SPIRITUAL GROWTH IN GIVING

The giving of monetary, human and material resources within the church is either token, faith, generous, or sacrificial, in that prioritized order:

• Token -- monetarily, when you look in your purse or wallet and just pull out something without forethought as to what God wants you to do or what is needed.

• Faith -- when you give either out of need or shortage, cutting back and doing without certain fleshly desires to give to kingdom work.

• Generous -- when you give from your surplus funds. (II Cor 8:13-14)

• Sacrificial -- when you give up something of great importance, something esteemed of great personal value to you in worship to God. (Luke 21:1-4, II Cor 8:2-5)

Many people are token and faith givers. Some even find no problem in giving generously. But very few people are sacrificial givers. Yet the rewards of sacrificial giving far outweigh those of the previous types of giving, combined. When you become a sacrificial giver, you'll easily be able to live in contentment, your faith in God will increase to greater trust in His ability to meet all your needs, and you'll experience a higher level in your walk with the Lord as you witness the power of His spiritual anointing on your money, possessions, and skills.

SACRIFICIAL GIVING

God does not expect a person to start sacrificially giving as a daily lifestyle. One must gradually grow through exercising all of the previous giving opportunities (token, faith, generous) before trusting God enough to give sacrificially with joy. The Lord even expects your sacrificial giving to grow from a little sacrifice to the giving of a greater sacrifice. In Scripture, we see such sacrifices taking place in the Old and New Testaments:

• Abraham's willingness to sacrifice Isaac (Gen 22:2, 12)

• Hannah's gift of Samuel to the Priesthood (I Sam 1:11, 24, 28;2:21)

• The widow of Zarephath's sacrifice of meal to Elijah (I Kings 17:8-16)

• The widow's mite (Mark 12:41-44)

• The sacrifice of all personal possessions by the early Church (Acts 4:32-37)

• Father God's sacrifice of His only Son, our Lord Jesus Christ (John 3:16)

Father God does not want us to sacrificially give to experience how it feels to go without the necessities of life; but instead, He wants us to see beyond the natural securities that we have learned to trust in. Thus, He wants us to take a spiritual "leap" to experience the rewards that He has set in motion for every sacrificial giver to experience if he will just try doing this "foolish thing" -- These rewards:

    • An increase in your faith that God will take care of your needs (Matt 6:19-33)

    • An increase in your ability to be patient & content (I Tim 6:6-8, James 1:3)

    • A spiritual anointing on the resources you manage for God (Deu 28:2-13, Isaiah 45:3)

CONNECTING WITH JESUS SACRIFICIALLY

I want you to see just how important it is for you to become a sacrificial giver. In Old Testament times people gave two general types of offerings (ofgs), animal offerings and meal offerings.* They were all given to make some reconciliation for sins (Ezekiel 45:15-17). They were basically broken down in the following manner:

O.T. SACRIFICE			NEW TESTAMENT
ANIMAL	FOR	TYPE	LIVING SACRIFICE

• Burnt Ofg
  herd
  flock
  goat
  fowl
	sins, trespasses	blood
		sacrifice
			J E S U S

• Peace Ofg
  herd
  flock
  goat
	thanksgiving	blood
		sacrifice
			J E S U S

MEAL			

• Meat/Meal Ofg
-- in pan/oven
  flour
  corn
  etc.
	sins, trespasses	oblation,
		bloodless
			CHRISTIANS

*footnote *(We'll leave off discussion of the jealousy, wood, and praise offerings for now for we are now studying a point of reference which connects sacrificial offerings with financial offerings. The sacrifice of praise is in musical worship; the jealousy offering concerns matters of marital fidelity, and the wood offering, a priestly order of preparing for the burning of sacrifices.)*

Now pay close attention to this analogy:
These three hebrew words translate "meat" in the law:

Lehem: *food, bread, grain, meal, fruit, meat, victuals*

Minhah: *food, meat, cereal, vegetable*

Okel: *food, meat, victuals*

These meat/meal sacrifices have nothing to do with blood, yet they are sacrifices. Our Lord Jesus Christ's precious blood, that He shed on the cross for us, took the place of all blood sacrifices. He's is the only blood covering we will ever need. Does that mean we should never have to give offerings anymore that cost us something of great value from the labor of our hands? Absolutely not! What we see in the above detailing is that we can never touch the hem of the blood sacrifice that the Lord Jesus Christ gave for us until we press beyond token, faith and generous giving to get to sacrificial giving of *that* which we treasure from the labor of our hands, our MONEY:

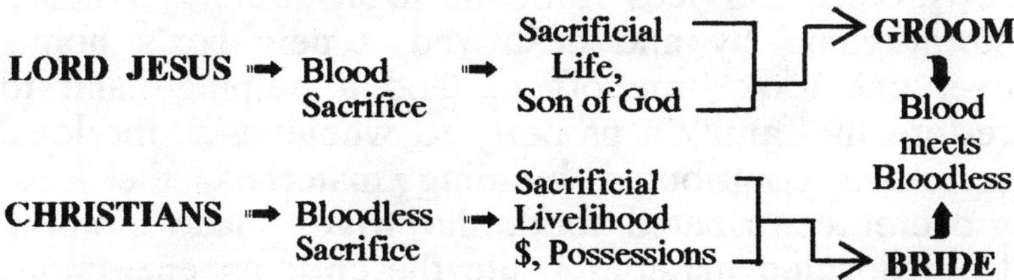

Just as the sacrificial blood Jesus shed on the cross replaces the O.T. blood sacrifices, so, only the <u>sacrificial money</u> that we freely give can replace the O.T. meal offerings. We have not even begun to connect with the significance of what Jesus' blood sacrifice did for us until we submit to give sacrificially of our finances back to God.

If you are already giving sacrificially but not prospering, your finances may be suffering from evil associations, a financial sin or a curse. For details, read those sections in chapters 2 and 4, respectively.

I'm a sacrificial giver of many years and have witnessed the mighty hand of God move supernaturally on my finances, possessions and skills. Part III, Chapter 15 shares my experiences in this glorious type of giving. You'll never realize what benefits you are missing till you begin to sacrificially give to the ministry work of Lord God Almighty.

For the remainder of this chapter, let us consider the general giving of money, time and resources as an aggregate part of our family's lifestyle.

GIVING OUT OF A PURE HEART

Years ago people used to barter: trade by exchanging one kind of goods or services for other goods or services without using money. Carpenters would barter construction work for food supplies from farmers. Farmers would barter grains and vegetables for medical services from the local doctor. When a storm came by and destroyed a neighbor's home, everyone took time off to lend a helping hand to restore the family's property to wholeness: the local merchant contributed building materials, the local grocerer contributed food, the wives made clothing from donated material while the children entertained each other. A person could not equitably assess the worth of his goods against the value of the services he was receiving; so, many times something was given above and beyond the actual value of that service rendered. But people didn't mind in those days. They weren't far from the times when American families exemplified Scriptural principles on giving in their home: " Give and ye shall receive...give and it shall be given unto you...if thy enemy be hungry, give him bread...give to the poor, and thou shalt have...give ye them to eat...give thyself wholly to them...it is more blessed to give than to receive".

It seems as if we could never go back to those days because everyone puts a dollar value on everything:

• This dress is too small. I've only worn it once so, I'll sell it.

• The attic is full of junk; I need a new patio set, a larger bed, a new dining room set, so, I'll have a garage sale.

• My old car is about to putter out. It's time for a new one. I think I'll put an ad in the paper.

Because we forget about the worth in giving away things of value, we miss out on receiving things of greater worth in return. Some of you are probably thinking, "What is she talking about? I give things to the Salvation Army." You do? What type of things? Someone gave me a garbage bag full of flattened, worn, smelly shoes. I was very insulted. They thought they were blessing me and would receive a blessing from God themselves in return. Yet the only blessing they were going to receive was probably two bags of worn shoes from somebody else. When I wanted to bless a young lady with some nice shoes who needed them, I took her to my closet, opened the door and said, *"Pick out a pair of shoes and take them."* She picked out my favorite pair. I was happy for her because she chose what she wanted among the best that I had to offer. When God touched another lady to give me several nice pairs of shoes, they were neatly packaged in their original boxes, some with the price tag still intact. The Lord tells us to "give good gifts" that's why I would not give anybody anything I would not wear, sit on, eat, or drive myself.

You can not open the windows of prosperity for your family until you learn to give with a pure heart. Everybody has time, skills, and money that they can sacrificially offer to God through what they do for ministry and for others as motivated by the Holy Spirit. Giving may not come naturally when you first get started. Don't make it complicated. Just start in your own backyard by giving your neighbor a hand. Once you start, the desire to help others will blossom within you.

IGNITING GIVING WITHIN THE FAMILY

Giving should be a regular part of your family budget that your children can actively participate in. When we gave our family console spinet piano to a church it was in tip-top shape. We missed it for the kids used to sing songs through the house as I played. God did not overlook our good deed; He replaced it 5 months down the road with a beautiful baby grand piano. When I gave a large amount of money to the church beyond my tithes and generous offerings, God provided my children and I with two nice cars, fully paid for. The Lord opened the hearts of our church members to go from house to house fulfilling home repair needs. We really enjoyed this time of bene-volence, especially when it was time to come to our house.

My children got so much in the spirit of giving that three Christmases they gave away more toys than they received. My children took good care of their toys, so much so that each year we'd pull them out only at Christmas time to watch the coal company trucks drive down the tracks to deliver coals to the neighborhood store, to see Mr. Whistle walk switching his hands as he whistled, to ride the hobby horse with the silky long tail, to play the old Sesame Street records and sing along with the story books, to play house with my daughter's nineteen dolls of all nationalities and colors and sharpen our wit with the many educational games and toys. We'd hoped some year to pass these well kept toys down to their children and my grandchildren. One year, just a few days before Christmas, learning of two little boys and their sister whose dad could not afford to buy them gifts, they parted with some of these well kept toys in mint condition. Another Christmas, they did the same, parting with a few more toys. My daughter and I, listening to a public appeal for dolls one Christmas, washed and pressed the clothing and freshly curled the hair of sixteen of her dolls. We left them all perched in rows in boxes lined up on the patio for pick-up in answer to the call for pretty dolls.

My brother and I made time to do street ministry to the poor. My children participated without complaining. We never turned down an offer to do music ministry. Sometimes it was on a flat-bed truck, sometimes in a store parking lot, other times in the shelters themselves where street people lived. There you would find my kids, my brother and I taking out time to minister and listen to the poor. It takes time to stop and listen.

OBEYING THE VOICE OF GOD

I get a lot of mail from organizations which minister overseas. I know we're told to be leery of such organizations which may not really feed the poor but fill their own pockets instead. I may receive a lot of mail from such organizations but I don't support all. Certain ones God leads me to intercede for, fast for, or just send five dollars here and there. Just be led by the Holy Spirit in your giving. (Refer to the section on

Giving for Scriptural wisdom on that subject.) Don't let skepticism keep you from following the lead of the Holy Spirit. One Christmas, when a ministry asked for coats, not money, for needy people in Russia, the Holy Spirit quickened to me that it was a genuine need. I gave them my Sunday coat.

Sometimes when God leads you to give you may not find a material or financial blessing to pin to it as a direct result of that sacrifice but there's either one already there or one on the way. I believe this with all my heart, that's why I happily obeyed when God led me to pay all the funeral and burial expenses of a poor widow woman's husband and when He led me to give even my now four year old baby grand piano to another church in need.

You must first be content with what you have before you can develop an attitude of giving your time and resources to others. Time is a precious commodity in our busy society. You can see this in the way the clock is centrally located at work, school and church. When I really wanted to give my time to God, I stopped wearing a wrist watch. Time actually seemed to slow down.

The church represents the voice of God. In giving, your church can ignite a spirit of giving in the congregation with the formulation of a "Helps Ministry". Therein, individuals who are willing to sacrifice the time and skill needed to help someone else in your church body who needs a service done (car repair, minor electrical work, sewing, carpentry, etc.) can furnish the manpower/woman power needed while the individual receiving the service furnishes his own parts and supplies. To make such a program effective, all who benefit from partaking of its services must sign up to also sacrifice a day to labor with their hands for someone else. Of course, you could accept monetary contributions from those who have more money than time or skill to contribute. Yet, after initiating such a program, you will soon discover that all of us have something to give. That's what Christ's sacrifice on the cross for us was all about, unselfishly giving.

II Corinthians 9:10 shows us the four benefits of unselfish giving:
"...(1) supplies seed to the sower ...(2) bread for food ...(3) supply and increase your store ...(4) enlarge the harvest of your righteousness". (Amplified)
All these benefits are yours just for obeying God's prioritized order in the multiplication process:
" Give and ye shall receive...give and it shall be given unto you...if thy enemy be hungry, give him bread...give to the poor, and thou shalt have...give ye them to eat...give thyself wholly to them...it is more blessed to give than to receive ".

THE MOTIVATIONAL GIFT OF GIVING

There is a special motivational gift of giving which God has bestowed upon certain individuals who are capable of handling large sums of funds for the Lord and moving major projects along for kingdom work in the ministry. Although all do not have this special anointing, God does expect all of us to give for it is the greatest form of worship that we can offer Him.

Before proceeding right into this unique gift, I want to fix in your mind clarity about the categorizing of the many gifts that God has bestowed upon His church body so you may understand that every spiritual gift is precious. Afterwards, we're just going to detail the attributes of the *Giving* gift because we are dealing with the broad subject of finances in this particular book.

Spiritual Gifts In General. We're familiar with the spiritual gifts detailed in I Cor 12:7-10 :

These are **manifestation gifts** given by one Spirit, the Holy Spirit, for the whole church body to profit.

Then there are **ministry gifts**, vocational gifts by which one is able to minister according to the anointing under which he is called to serve the church body God has placed him in. Ephesians 4:11 lists these as: *"...apostles...prophets...evangelists...pastors...teachers"*

Now let's direct our focus to the group of gifts under which *Giving* is categorized in the Bible, what many refer to as **motivational gifts.** These gifts are recognized as such because they motivate us to do service for the Lord Jesus Christ by the working of that self same Spirit, the Holy Spirit. They are detailed in Romans 12:6-8 as:

Understanding Your Gift. Somehow, God saw that He could trust me with the motivational gift of giving. I learned through varied church instruction how to see all resources coming through my hands as they really are: God's, not mine. The Lord then taught me how to be a steward rather than an owner of His money through many years of financial resource challenges and opportunities to development wisdom in the management of resources on the job and at home. Through these challenges and opportunities, the Lord brought me to a place of patience (to learn to wait for the Lord's counsel), thriftiness and contentment and caution. The Lord even showed me the importance of giving high quality gifts not just my leftovers or worn out items. I learned how God works through an opportunity of time when He wanted to bestow supernatural funds through me for a particular ministry

70

need. You see, all monies that God gives you is not for you; some funds He passes through you because He knows you will distribute it according to His will when the other existing avenues are either unreliable or spiritually hindered for some reason (i.e. unresolved curses, sins or lack of faith existing when the situation requires more in touching the spiritual realm to access God's supply.)

The Lord also taught me the benefit in giving quietly, without notice. It gives the glory to Him, not you, for all the blessings that He has bestowed on that ministry or need. It also keeps those away who only want to be a friend of your money and not of you. One time when the Lord directed me to quietly give some very expensive material possessions to a lady whom I hardly knew, she was so excited that she told the whole church the next Sunday, in my presence. I guess I should have been proud of myself for obeying God but instead, I was so disappointed in the fact that she didn't give credit to God that I just wanted to run out of the church. I didn't look at anyone else for the remainder of the service and spent much time in fear of what the Lord thought. She later came to me, privately, to ask forgiveness, which mended my concerns. You see, a motivated giver is always concerned about pleasing God in the way he gives for he knows he's just a steward over that which is God's:

"...He that is greatest among you shall be your servant. And who-soever shall exalt himself shall be abased; and he that shall hum-ble himself shall be exalted." (Matt 23:11-12)

Understanding God's Timing. A person with this unique gift is very concerned about being punctual with his giving. I've found that when God wants you to distribute something or help in some way, He has a special window of time: it could be immediately or He

71

may just give you a fore-notice because you may have to set up some special arrangements or coordinations involving others. Sometimes such windows begin with a spiritual revelation from God that we must present to the recipient within an appointed time and in return receive information from them. Sometimes skepticism may surface as to your true intentions, which is logical to presume considering the amount of hypocrisy in the church today. Yet, because a motivated giver is not pushy, he will let the matter lay, for if the Lord doesn't intervene in the appointed recipient's actions there could be a lost opportunity for supernatural provision in a needy area that later will have to be dealt with through the normal world system channels of long term financing.

The motivation to give must be initiated by God and must be without self-glory. As you answer your calling from God to give motivated by Him, you must become selfless and focused on Him and not the giving situation. Sometimes you will have to spend time and resources on a person who is totally ungrateful of your efforts. You will have to get out of the mode of thinking, "Well, what will people think or say?" because you are giving to please God and not people.

Learning To Receive. A motivational giver may find it hard to receive from others until broken by God. God had me to even give away many of my best clothes, business suits and stylish shoes in order to put me in a position to receive from others He had motivated to give to me. (You can always tell if a person had really been motivated by God to give to you because He will only motivate them to give you good quality items without public awareness.)

Learning To Tap Into Favor. Sometimes God will put you in a serious situation where you know He is tugging at your spirit to help someone yet you have no liquid funds. Here, He will give you an intuitive awareness of His direction. Around 11:30 pm one Thursday night I found myself cuddling a bewildered young Christian mother of three little ones in my arms whose husband had just died days prior but who had not been properly laid to rest because she had no means to pay his burial expenses. The mortician wanted a retainer fee and the balance paid within thirty days. The Lord prompted me to call two of my banks in another state. I called one at this late hour and sure enough I could talk to a real live bank teller at this late hour! She prepared the necessary documentation over the phone and said I'd receive the funds within seven days. Additionally, God does not leave you burdened for your obedience to Him. By the time the first payment was due on the loan God provided funds that I was able to pay off the balance, in full, on that very day.

Applying Business Acumen. Individuals with the motivational gift of giving are shrewd business-men. They don't give funds directly to the God-sent individuals but either secure the needed item or confer with the business with whom that God-sent individual deals. You see, motivated givers are not "easy takers". They are considered quite stingy by those who know them well. Motivational givers are "serious tight wads". They are made so by the Lord because they are not to respond to financial pleas coming from individuals or ministries who just approach them out of need but only to those God has sent to them. These are individuals or ministry work that the Lord already fore-prepared them (through words of wisdom, words of knowledge, discerning of spirits, etc.) to consider. And then, after that, they wait on other confirmations from the Lord. You see, some people are in some financial situations because of mismanagement of funds, sins, or other self-inflicted reasons that must be worked out between that person, or that ministry, and God as He lets them wander in their financial wilderness, unnoticed by even a room filled with motivational givers because there is no mercy (compassion for their carelessness with God's funds) or grace (unmerited favor).

Applying Spiritual Acumen. Although motivational givers are prompted by God to minister to some individuals, the main calling of such gifted ones is to support ministry work. In any event, the complete fulfillment of their calling to meet a ministry need includes submission, by that ministry, to any resource management counsel God inspires the motivated giver to give them. For instance, where there exists a problem of spiritual origin unaware to the ministry being helped, say, a witchcraft curse on that ministry's finances and the ministry refuses to deal with the breaking of the curse, the salvation or removal of that witch (if he/she is a member of that ministry), or other measures of separation from satanic strongholds, God will not allow that motivational giver to undergird that ministry's financial need. The Lord will not allow His funds to be poured down an opened hole. What has been brought to the light must be dealt with and what has not been dealt with remains in the dark:

"And the times of this ignorance God winked at: but now commandeth all men everywhere to repent." (Acts 17:30)

"And have no fellowship with the unfruitful works of darkness, but rather reprove them....but all things that are reproved are made manifested by the light: for whatsoever doth make manifest is light.....wherefore be ye not unwise, but understanding what the will of the Lord is." (Ephesians 5:11-17)

A final word of caution: a ministry may approach you with a genuine financial ministry need but you may not be the giver that God has motivated to meet that particular ministry need. Sometimes, God purposes certain motivational givers to be used in certain ministry situations either within or without the body; so, whereas a need is genuine it may not be your calling to undergird it. The purpose of the motivational giver is NOT to interfere with the requirement for ALL within the body to give faithfully, generously, and sacrificially. When this occurs because parishioners are aware that motivational givers are present within the congregation, God will not initiate a motivation to stir up the gifted one but will only allow this gifted one to function as a typical Christian, giving a basic free will offering.

"For I mean not that other men be eased, and ye burdened." (II Cor 8:13)

"EVERY MAN according as he purposeth in his heart, so let him give; not grudgingly, or of necessity: for God loveth a cheerful giver." (II Cor 9:7)

Giving Resources Instead of Money. A motivational giver does not have to be rich in order to be motivated to give. When he no longer has anything to give in a monetary way, the motivated giver still knows how to find resources to give because it's his nature. When God chose to decrease me naturally that I might increase supernaturally He commanded me to sell my goods, liquidate my funds and distribute to ministry work and specified poor. I no longer had the funds to contribute to various ministry work. For a while I sent a dollar here and there to some ministries. Then God opened the door of opportunity to give within my existing means. I thanked the Lord for these opportunities and pursued them. These opportunities:

• Sending used Bibles to Africa.

• Sending used shoes in good condition (with socks and bar soap) to Romania. (I sent them my best pair of dress shoes.)

• Sending winter coats to Russia.

Giving Disciplines. After reading this section, if you find that you have the motivational gift of giving, I caution you with the following advice:

(1). Don't use your giving to control ministry work. God directs you to fulfill needs without putting pressure on the ministry or person He has directed you to bless.

(2). Don't be pushy. Just present to the ministry or individual what God said to you. If it's a true need already existing, your coming to them will only confirm what God said to you. Let them reject or accept the opportunity; however, God's window of opportunity remains open for a certain period of time. When people/ministry sees you give without strings attached or possessiveness, it's a sure sign to them that you are truly God's messenger to them.

Budding Givers, Not Yet Discovered. Sometimes you will meet others who have this same gift but they are not being used by God because of their disobedience or lack of knowledge concerning the purpose for and operation of such a gift. They didn't know they were a giver but they now know because, after seeing God use you, they can identify with the same motivations you display.

Recycling Abundance! When you give as God directs you, He will cause you to then receive more abundance to have more to give:

"Give and [gifts] will be given you, good measure, pressed down, shaken together and running over will they pour into [the pouch formed by] the bosom [of your robe and used as a bag]. For with the measure you deal out - that is, with the measure you use when you confer benefits on others - it will be measured back to you." (Luke 6:38) Amplified

What Is Your Gift? The Bible tells us that spiritual gifts are without repentance, so you already have a gift bestowed upon you from the Lord. What is yours? It may not be giving, but if it is, you need to ask God to place you in a position to receive knowledge about it and then give you opportunities to exercise this gift.

Don't let the Lord return finding you doing many good works and He says, *"Depart from me, I know ye not..."* because you are busy doing everything but what God has called you to do. If that motivational gift that God has placed in you is giving and God has bestowed a special anointing upon you to handle large sums of funds and move major projects along for kingdom work in the ministry, will He find you faithful and resourceful in your stewardship or will He find you an unprofitable servant whom He will cast into outer darkness?

CHAPTER 9

WISDOM FROM SOLOMON ON HANDLING FINANCES

INTRODUCTION

It is recorded in I Kings 4:32 that King Solomon wrote 3,000 Proverbs and 1,005 songs. The Bible records many of these proverbs in the Books of Proverbs and Ecclesiastes and many of the songs in the Canticles, better known as the Song of Solomon. Many of these proverbs address finances in one form or another. Although Solomon has a lot of wisdom to impart to us on the handling of finances in both books, each book takes a different slant on addressing the subject of wealth and its fruits. We will look at these two views of dealing with finances because it is God's desire that we learn from a person's failures as well as his successes. Solomon's spiritual state when walking in the statutes of God manifested spiritual wisdom which is imparted to us in Proverbs. When Solomon walked in a degenerate state he continued to manifest wisdom but predominantly human wisdom, that which is seen through the eyes of one who leads a fleshly oriented lifestyle. First let's understand what it means to operate in spiritual wisdom vs human wisdom, for both are gifts from God .

THE TWO-SIDED VIEW OF SOLOMON'S WISDOM

God gave King Solomon immense wisdom: Spiritual wisdom, which is divinely imparted to our spirit man, and human wisdom, which can be learned experi-entially or vicariously. Either wisdom, once received, can then be retained and applied. The wisdom Solomon imparts in Proverbs was received while he was walking in fellowship with the Spirit of God. His spirit man dominated his actions; his soul interpreted that wisdom into knowledge and understanding, then his flesh followed the heart of his spirit man. Proverbs gives the reader a positive look at walking through life in the fear of God, subordinating pleasures and fleshly cares. (To receive a deeper understanding of this revelation, refer to the "Your Finances" chart in Chapter 1, The Spirituality of Money.)

The collection of wise sayings Solomon imparts to the reader in Ecclesiastes (The Preacher) lays before us a shift in his frame of reference as he is now fallen from divine fellowship to a backslidden state. (God is always moving forward. If you aren't moving with Him, you're sliding backwards -- Hosea 4:16.) The concentration is mainly on looking at the adverse side of wisdom; yet, there exists sprinklings of some spiritual truths peppered throughout various sections of this book (Eccles 8:12). Here, his flesh dominated his actions and view of life; his soul interpreted this flesh-generated human wisdom into knowledge and understanding which we still operate in, even today, when we walk outside the will of God. You see, Solomon had extracted this human wisdom from experiences anyone could have had, residing in a dominant position of "kingly wealth, fame, and power".

Don't think for one moment that everyone that's walking outside the will of God is a dunce! Look at the world's finance tycoons who run Wall Street, the money-making behind-the-scene geniuses in motion picture productions, the brains behind the marketing of professional sporting events, computer program geniuses; these all operate out of fleshly human human wisdom that has nothing to do with a spiritual walk with God. Yet, it exists because God ordained that we have both types of wisdom. Thus, we can learn something of financial value from Solomon under both conditions.

EVALUATING THE THEMES

All themes in both Proverbs and Ecclesiastes lead to viewpoints of life gained through experience while having wealth, power, riches and fame; yet, lessons from experiences while walking in the spirit generate more balanced advice to the reader than that generated through times of walking in the flesh:

PROVERBS	ECCLESIASTES
• Predominantly Spiritual Wisdom	• Predominantly Human Wisdom
• Gives the Adverse & Converse	• Gives Only the Adverse
- negative & positive view of life shown	- negative view of life of shown
- causes spirit of reader to drop but rise again	- causes spirit of reader to drop & stay down
- leaves prov on high note	-leaves prov on a low note
= uplifting	= depressing/oppressing
• Concentration/Tone:	• Concentration/Tone:
◆--Humility	◆--Vanity, Vexation of Spirit
◆--Love of Wisdom	◆--Awareness of Wisdom
◆--Mercy, Giving	◆--Self-Centeredness
◆--Love	◆--Hate, Despair
◆--Blessing	◆--Curses
◆--Not Pleasure Focused	◆--Pleasure Focused
◆--Fear of God	◆--Fear of Circumstances
◆--Loves Instruction	◆--Hates Instruction
◆--Inheritance Encouraged	◆--Inheritance Discouraged
◆--Trust in God	◆--Trust in Flesh
◆--Life, preoccupied	◆--Death, preoccupied

PROVERBS: WISDOM LEARNED FROM SPIRITUAL OBEDIENCE

The Character of Proverbs' Wisdom:

• Divinely spiritual, plus human common sense.
• Representative of the Holy Spirit. (The spirit of wisdom, 8:22-30; also Exod 28:3, Deu 34:9, Eph
   1:17)
• Representative of a female because she reproduces
   (8:2, 3; 9:2, 3, 4).   (That's why many people
   confuse the loose woman in verse 16 with the
   the female rendering of the spirit of wisdom in
   verse 4, identical Scriptures.)
• Based on the fear of the Lord. (16 times in Prov, only
   5 times in Eccles)

• Produces the following in a person in matters dealing
   with finances, wealth and prosperity--
◆--He will value wisdom, instruction and knowledge
   over money for he knows that true treasures follow wisdom. (8:10-11, 19-20; 20:15)
◆--He will inherit substance and treasure. (8:21; 15:6;
   21:20)
◆--His diligence will make him rich. (10:4; 11:24;
   13:4)
◆--His riches will become a strong city. (10:15)
◆--His labor will produce life and increase for him and
   his household. (10:16; 11:28; 13:11)
◆--He will walk in the blessing of the LORD. (10:22;
   22:9; 28:20)
◆--He will always use a just weight in dealing financially with others. (11:1; 16:11; 20:10, 23;
   20:14)
◆--He will not sign for the security of another's debt.
   (11:15; 17:18; 20:16)
◆--His giving makes him rich. (13:7, 19:17; 21:26)
◆--He will receive instruction. (13:18)
◆--He will leave an inheritance for his grandchildren.
   (13:22; 9:14)

◆--He will have many friends. (14:20; 19:4)
◆--He will find profit in all his labor. (14:23a)
◆--His riches will be a crown for him. (14:24a)
◆--He gives to the poor. (19:17; 21:13; 21:26; 22:9; 31:20)
◆--He will pay his tithes and vows. (20:25)
◆--He will not lie or steal. (21:6-7)
◆--He will not covet. (21:26)
◆--He will not love pleasure. (21:17)
◆--Humility (22:4)
◆--The Fear of the LORD (22:4)
◆--The character of a ruler (22:7)
◆-- A bountiful eye (22:9)
◆--He will never come to want (never lack). (22:16)
◆--He will not labor to be rich. (23:4-5)
◆--He will not be a drunkard or glutton. (23:21a)
◆--He will not be slothful. (23:21b; 24:30-34)
◆--He knows riches don't last forever and plans accordingly. (27:24)
◆--He will not charge interest. (28:8)
◆--He will not increase his substance through unjust gain. (28:8)
◆--He will prosper from confessing and forsaking his sins. (28:13)
◆--He will not haste to be rich. (28:20, 22)
◆--He desires not vanity, lies, poverty, nor riches. (30:8-9)
◆--He pleads the cause of the poor and needy. (31:8-9)
◆--He considers before he buys. (31:16)
◆--He knows how to turn the works of his hand into wealth. (31:24)
◆--His hands are fruitful. (31:31)

ECCLESIASTES: WISDOM LEARNED
FROM CARNAL VANITIES

The Character of Ecclesiastes' Wisdom:
• Based on unhappy conditions of a backslider
• Addresses Life Under The Sun
• Doesn't go beyond death in his discourse
• Derived out of Vanity
> vanity, Hebrew: *hebel, habel, habal* (Strong's
> Concordance)
> --emptiness   --transitory
> --unsatisfactory   --to lead astray
> vanity = pride = Luciferian spirit

• Derived out of "Vexation of Spirit"
> vexation = cursed

The Vexations of Solomon's Spirit in Ecclesiastes. These vexations were curses sent by God upon a man who knew His commandments, statutes, and His voice, but would not obey Him. Solomon fell into this category during these soulish and carnal days, separated from spiritual direction (retaining only that spiritual wisdom which remained in his human intellect from the days when he did walk with the LORD) because of his rejection of God's commandments. Read it for yourself in Deuteronomy 28:15-20:

> *"...if thou will not hearken unto the voice of the LORD thy God* ***...all these curses*** *shall come upon thee, and overtake thee:.... thee:...the LORD shall send upon thee cursing,* ***vexation,*** *and and rebuke, in all that thou settest thine hand unto for to do..... because of the wickedness of thy doings, whereby thou hast hast forsaken me."*

Of the ten Scriptures in Ecclesiastes which specifically say Solomon was experiencing, "vexation of spirit" five of these address financial matters. It would be-

hoove us to pay close attention to these:
1. The works of his hands now yielded no profit for he
      had spent it on pleasures. (2:1-11)
2. The work of his hands was grievous to him. (2:17)
3. He now gathered and heaped up to give to those
      who were good before God. (2:26)
4. He even alluded to the present day fact that God
      gives peace when ONE person works outside
      the home (a handful, with quietness) for vexa-
      tion comes within the household when both
      husband and wife (both hands full) work tra-
      vail) outside the home. (4:6)
5. When he used his financial resources to fulfill his
      wandering desires, he vexed his spirit for de-
      sires are never satisfied (6:9). Wandering de-
      sires are based on what it available but you
      don't have it in your possession, yet; like ivory,
      apes, peacocks from foreign lands and Egyptian
      made chariots. (I Kings 10:22-29)

The Character of Ecclesiastes' Wisdom: (cont'd)
•Produces the following adverse concentration in a
person when dealing with finances, wealth and pros-
perity--
◆--Concern about profit from labor (1:3)
◆--Discouragement: "...no new thing..." (1:9)
◆--Concern about vain works and experiences:
      =the vanities of materialism and pleasures (1:2,
            14; 2:1, 11, 15,17, 19, 21, 2:23, 26; 3:19;
            4:4, 7, 8, 16; 5:7, 10; 6:2, 4, 9,11; 7:6,
            15; 8:10, 14; 9:9; 11:8, 9)
◆--Vexation of spirit (1:14, 17; 2:11,17, 22, 26; 4:4, 6,
      16; 6:9)
◆--He will see no profit. (2:11)
◆--He will see his work as grievous. (2:17)
◆--He will hate life. (2:17)

◆--He will hate giving the fruit of his labor as inheritance to his children.(2:18-19)
◆--He will despair within his heart of all his labor. (2:20)
◆--Preoccupation with thoughts about wickedness and sin. (3:16)
◆--Preoccupation with thoughts about the power of the oppressor. (4:1)
◆--Preoccupation with thoughts about evil work. (4:3)
◆--His eyes will never be satisfied with riches. (4:7-8; 5:10, 6:7)
◆--He will see no end of generations of people. (4:15-16)
◆--He will see perishing riches. (5:13-14)
◆--He will see lost inheritance. (5:14)
◆--He will see those with riches with no power to eat. (6:1-2) (yet at times, there is power to eat 5:18-19)
◆--Concern about vanity and a name covered with darkness. (6:3-5)
◆--He will see life as a shadow. (6:12)
◆--**A good view!** (He will see wisdom as profitable; life; a defense greater than that of money, which doesn't give life. 7:11-12)
◆--He will see one man ruling over another to his own hurt. (8:9)
◆--He will focus on mirth, pleasure: eat, drink, be merry. (8:15; 2:24; 3:13; 5:18; 9:7) (note: Epicureans used this theme later in N.T. times, a self-indulgent philosophical group of Athens that confronted Paul; idol worshipers; believed the mind dies with the body.)
◆--He will see one event happening to all. (9:3)
◆--He will see man's heart as full of evil and madness. (9:3)

◆--He will see death as the end: after life, go to the dead. (9:3)
◆--He will place his hope in the living; for the memory of the dead is forgotten. (9:4-6)
◆--**A good view!** (He will see marriage lasting til death.) (9:9)
◆--He will see time & chance, happening to all. (9:11)
◆--He will see the wisdom of a poor man as being despised. (9:15-16)
◆--He will see the evil of fools in high places, rich in low. (10:5-6)
◆--He will see money as answering all things. (10:19)
◆--**A good view!** He will acknowledge the laws of sowing and reaping. (11:1, 6)
◆--He will see days of darkness. (11:7-8)
◆--He will see death as fearful. (12:1-7)

EMPTY PROFIT FROM LIFE'S LABOR SEEN IN THE FINAL DEATH ANALOGY IN ECCLESIASTES

The final picture of death that King Solomon paints at the end of Ecclesiastes shows that wealth could not change the unhappy departure of a restless man, *"....when they shall be afraid of that which is high (God) and fears shall be in the way...."*. His preoccupation with the follies of the labor for money only emphasized his awareness of its natural aspects, failing to see its spiritual qualities and applications under the sun -- qualities a spiritual man would not have overlooked (see chapter 1).

Although death is a preoccupation throughout Ecclesiastes, Solomon's discourse on man's final departure from the days under the sun is so filled with symbolism that the death subject there is not even noticed as he gracefully uses various analogies to describe the aged decaying of man's body (12: 1-7).

Yet, the description of this vain fellow's eyes, on his death bed, told of a life of financial woes:

> darkened eyes = heaviness of spirit
> brightened eyes = less burdensome spirit

When we are not regenerated by the presence of the Holy Spirit, as would be the man walking in spiritual wisdom, our eyes can tell the story of our lives, our past woes, our current condition, and even reveal the presence of demon spirits.

It is sad for a man to just live for the pleasures he can experience under the sun, for when his days are nearing an end, his spirit is truly vexed for then he can only see the dust returning to the earth and his spirit returning to God. To him, it is, *"vanity of vanities..... ...all is vanity."* Let us learn from Ecclesiastes that these are indeed words of truth for they speak of what a carnal man actually experiences when he falls from God and yet continues to live on. Yet, because even in his carnal state Solomon knows that God is supreme (just as King Cyrus and King Nebuchadnezzar knew), he concludes with a statement that even the vexed and backslidden can admit: that the whole duty of man is to fear God, who is the judge of every secret thing.

THE BOTTOM LINE ON FINANCIAL WISDOM

You can only use the wisdom in Ecclesiastes in conjunction with the wisdom in Proverbs for not until then will you obtain a "wholesome picture" of what God blessed Solomon with when He ordained Solomon to walk in BOTH. If you can grasp this point you will never again say, *"money answereth all things"* for you will then be enlightened as a spiritual man to know that money does not answer all the bondages and captivities people have placed themselves under because of their pursuit of silver and gold rather than the true riches of life, while under the sun.

"[Instead of repairing the breaches, the officials] make a feast for laughter, serve wine to cheer life, and depend on [tax] money to answer for all of it."   (Eccles 10:19)   Amplified

I pray that you have been enlightened from this study of the two-sided view of the wisdom of Solomon as presented in the books of Proverbs and Ecclesiastes.

CHAPTER 10

TRUSTING GOD TO MEET YOUR NEEDS

TRUST

*"It is better to trust in the LORD than to put
confidence in man...(or)...princes. Ps 118:8-9*

Sometimes when we get into a financial tight spot, we get caught up in the mentality that a second job for a short period of time will solve the problem; however, later, we find ourselves in financial bondage. Why do we strap ourselves and tie up our time so? Because we see money as our source, not God. That second job will also change you:

-- It will steal your time away from your family,

-- It will steal your quiet time alone with God.

-- It will make you acquire more debt, feeling you have extra money to spend.

-- You'll develop a dependency on *it* when you originally took it to satisfy a temporary need. That's a snare (Prov 29:25).

Psalm 127:2 says, *"It is vain for you to rise up early, to sit up late, to eat the bread of sorrows: for so he giveth his beloved sleep."* If we would daily spend the proper time it takes to prepare for, drive to and from our main job; eat, fellowship and individually counsel with our family members; spend quality quiet time with the LORD before the day begins and again before retiring; and to get a full night's rest, there would be no additional time to work additional jobs. If you are already in that predicament, you will have to continue for a while until you close out some debt, permanently. Then begin to decrease your lifestyle.

You may probably be thinking by now that if you had the money of your neighbor who is a lawyer, banker, etc. you wouldn't have all these bills; yet, many times even those types of individuals tend to build an increasing trust in their funds. That's why the LORD even tells the rich in this world not to trust in riches. In fact, He calls them *uncertain riches*. Their focus is to be on doing good works, distributing to the poor, and being sociable (reachable).

If you purpose not to get caught up in the financial bondage tightrope, God will meet your needs. When you discipline yourself to trust Him for the impossible, He will grant you Favor, Contentment, Patience, and Spiritual Provision.

FAVOR

Did you know that there are other rewards which outweigh the need to have money in your hands? One of these is Favor. In Luke 16: 5-7 we see a steward who called upon all those who owed his lord large sums of debt but he wrote off most of the debt (50% for one debtor, 20% for another). This steward was in the position to collect debt from pledges; being judged by his lord as one who wasted goods, this steward gained the favor of the debtor. You are probably in the position to be called a debtor rather than a lender; yet, the lesson you really gain here is that if you show favor to others, those who lord over you will show you favor. Notice how this steward's master who had once called him "wasteful" now "commends" him. The steward gained the lord's favor. Other examples of favor are found in Joseph's relationship with Potiphar (Gen 39:6) and Daniel's relationship with King Darius (Dan 6:1-3). How do you obtain God's divine favor?

• Diligently seek to do good. (Prov 11:27, 12:2)
• Be Christ-like. (Luke 2:52)
• Increase your understanding. (Prov 13:15)

- Be righteous. (Prov 14:9, Ps 5:12)
- Have mercy on others. Be truthful. (Prov 3:3-4)
- Seek the favor of the one in charge. (Prov 19:12)
- Put your trust in God. (Psalm 5:11-12)

Many times God grants divine favor when we respond to a need. Yet, we must initiate an action to open the door. Remember the widowed Christian mom (in Chapter 8) the LORD prompted me to help with her husband's burial expenses? I contacted the second bank on the next day by telephone, for she needed the retainer fee immediately. The following morning, I arose early to drive to that out-of-state bank, to arrive as soon as it opened. When I approached the first teller I saw, explaining why I was there, the bank manager arose from her glass-walled office and approaching the teller said, *"I've already taken care of Mrs. Britt."* She handed me a sealed envelope and wisked me out of the door in seconds! I was on the road and had returned to my state of departure, placing the retainer fee in the hands of the mortician late that same morning. When I opened the envelope to glance at the signature block, it read "pre-approved". Not only did that bank manager make me feel as though I was their largest depositor (which I wasn't) but I had a true experience of what it meant to have ultimate divine favor.

CONTENTMENT

I Timothy 6:8 says, *"And having food and raiment let us be therewith content."* Contentment is a choice of your will, not necessarily because it makes you happy but because it is in the will of God. It's trusting God for tomorrow as you live for today.

PATIENCE

"Wait on the LORD: be of good courage, and he shall strengthen thine heart: wait, I say, on the LORD." (Psalm 27:14)

It takes patience to wait on the LORD, especially today with the "hurry-up," "I can't wait," "me-me-me," "now-now-now" mentality. We've let the world system mold us to become this way through such things as fast foods, drive-in businesses, charge cards, ATM cards, cellular telephones, etc. Having patience takes discipline and discipline takes time.

It took patience for David to fight to get the kingdom when God had previously told him he would be king; many people died in battle; many years passed.

It took patience for Joseph to wait for years in jail, imprisoned by the lies of Potiphar's wife, and yet he still developed the wisdom it took to become second only to Pharaoh. (Couldn't you imagine yourself saying, "Did you forget about me LORD?")

Daniel's long night's stay in the lion's den, again jailed falsely, was a minute by minute wait with Daniel wondering when the LORD would deliver him: in one hour? in five hours? in eight hours? Yet the LORD waited until the next morning to set him free. Patience.

During the days of the four gospels, the Lord Jesus Christ was God in the flesh, the Living Word that came to dwell among us. He could have offered us salvation in any other painless, short-cut way, but He patiently lived thirty three years, waiting through the years it would take to grow up from a babe to a child to a young adult to a man (Son of God) that would have to be whipped, spit upon, pierced, and nailed to a rugged cross for our sins. He patiently bled sacrificial blood for us.

Paul waited out a thorn in the flesh - for how long, we know not - but he was consoled in the

LORD's response, *"...My grace is sufficient for thee: for my strength is made perfect in weakness..."* to which Paul responded, *"Therefore, I take pleasure in infirmities, in reproaches, in necessities, in persecutions, in distresses for Christ's sake: for when I am weak, then am I strong"* (II Corinthians 12:9-10). Patience.....

Patience....yet, you want God to get you out of debt right now when it took you years to get in........?

Learning to go through rather than borrow, file bankruptcy, or just evade your bills won't teach you patience. Only disciplined stewardship will.

SPIRITUAL PROVISION

The manna that God provided to the children of Israel in the wilderness was spiritual provision that was to be eaten without complaining. When God stopped this provision, they had to plant their own food.

We all must go through financial wildernesses at some point in our Christian walk. Yet, your spiritual prosperity, which is tied in with God, will come. When you are then walking in prosperity, after coming out of a financial wilderness that God has supernaturally sustained you in, do you now start buying for yourself items you prefer in clothing, cars, and other material possessions or do you continue with the same means of provisions you are continuing to receive?

After my spiritual promotion from God, people noticed that I started dressing differently: wore new dresses, new suits, etc. Some looked as if to say, *"She's rich, she can afford it."* Others,who knew these items were actually given to me, raised the question to me, *"Here you are now walking in prosperity and still wear used clothes or clothes others picked out for you."* I asked the LORD Jesus was this wrong? He spoke to my spirit, *"When manna ceased from heaven, they planted. When people stop giving, you need to start buying because your supply will have ceased."* Who knows the opportunity you may be cutting off from someone else whom God is teaching to give to you that they too may prosper? So, when do you stop walking in spiritual provision?   When God stops supplying it.   Remember, your prosperity is tied in with the LORD.

STEWARDSHIP VERSUS OWNERSHIP

"Beware that thou forget not the LORD thy God...And thou say in thine heart, My power and the might of mine hand hath gotten me this wealth. But thou shalt remember the LORD thy God: for it is He that giveth thee power to get wealth, that He may establish His covenant....."
Deuteronomy 8:11, 17-18

When we hear the truths of God concerning His finances it is like finding a perfect jewel under an unturned stone!   We are first humbled and broken in spirit by our willfull, sinful abuse of that which really belongs to Him. All along, we thought He only held us accountable for the 10% tithe not realizing that *that* part was so sacred that it wasn't even a choice for us to consider even touching that holy portion. The 10% was sacred, set apart from the very beginning. The 90% is the part He let us hold for Him, to manage it, reproduce it and multiply it while He's away that when He returns He may find a great increase by our faithful investment of His finances and material possessions. How could we forget that even in Scripture the Lord Jesus Christ showed us we don't even own the 90%? It's all His! We've just been managing it for Him!

Steward. A house distributor, managing and overseeing property and possessions which belong to someone else.

Let's dissect and analyze the teachings of the Parable of the Talents (Matt 25:14-30). Notice the bold-faced words:

    "*...a **man** traveling into a far country, ...*" (that's God)

    "*...called his own **servants**...*" (that's us)

    "*...delivered unto them **His** goods...*" (that's God)

    "*...his **Lord's** money...*" (that's God)

    "*...hid **thy** talent.....*" (that's God) (Notice that the servant DID at least hide it.

    "*...there **thou** hast that is **thine**....*" (That's God)

    "*...**wicked......slothful......**" (that's those of us who abused it -- spent amiss, no investments, no giving to poor, just fun, pleasures, the best of everything.)

    "*...**exchangers**.....*" (bankers)

    "*...**mine** own with usury....*" (That's God's, with interest)

    "*..hath, shall be given ....**abundance**....*" (That's to those of us who rightfully invested and increased as stewards rather than owners.)

    "*...hath not, shall be taken away....that which he hath.....**outer darkness**.....*" (That's a curse to those of us who waste the 90%)

Notice that everyone received something from the Master. What have you done with what little increase you first had? Planted it or wasted it? That "outer darkness" could just be the low income job you always manage to get, the bills that always seem to mount up, the items you buy which always seem to get easily damaged, stolen, lost, or just deteriorate rapidly, for no reason, or maybe that new automobile which always ends up being the only "lemon" on the car lot.

Your stewardship is very important to God. He wants you to see the finances that He has placed in your hands as something He has only given you to manage because it is His, all His. The application of your stewardship starts with your accepting and applying what the Word of God says about discipline in managing these resources. This book has given you a start in putting those Scriptural references into modern-day situational applications. The Scriptural principles in Appendix D will be even more of a biblical asset as you seek to find the heart of God in resource management. Then comb your Bible for a thorough Scriptural search as the Holy Spirit inspires you to advance forward as a seasoned steward of God's financial resources.

May I close Part I with this short Summary?

"12 Sure Ways the Bible Promises Will Return Riches & Wealth to You From God"

1. Separate your life completely unto God's will.
   (Genesis 13:2, 14-17)
2. Associate with prosperous people.
   (Genesis 39:2-5)
3. Be people-focused rather than self-focused.
   (I Kings 3:9-13)
4. Make God your strength, not trust in riches.
   (Psalm 52:7)
5. FEAR THE LORD.
   (Psalm 112:1-3)
6. Become a diligent, hard worker.
   (Proverbs 10:4)

7. Answer the Calling God has for your life, regardless the price.   *(Isaiah 45:3)*
8. Become a generous giver.
(Luke 6:38)
9. Be rich toward God; don't hoard possessions for
yourself.   *(Luke 12:16-21)*
10. Sacrificially give up your possessions when motivated by God to do so; distribute to the poor.
(Luke 18:22-23)
11. Become a sacrificial giver out of your own will.
(Acts 4:34-37)
12. Be rich in good works.
(I Timothy 6:18)

If after reading PART I you feel like you've just finished a Bible Study Course, GREAT! It is time to stop separating Finances from its Scriptural roots. They are inseparable. The truth was established by God and it still resides in Him. Now that we've searched the Scripture for its foundational wisdom in Finances, let's learn how to apply these wise principles.

PART II:

KINGDOM LIVING: THE APPLICATION OF A SOUND BUDGET

§

CHAPTER 11

SOUND BUDGET DOCTRINE

BUDGET COMMITMENTS

After you've made your financial covenants with the Lord, you need to move on to establishing a sound budget that is biblically prioritized and purged from financial sins, curses, and ignorances. Only after setting up this Scripturally based money management plan called a budget will you realize that it isn't how much money you make, but how you handle the funds you do have, that makes the difference in your living flexibility.

Handling your funds with accountability will afford you a good credit rating. Having a good credit rating will afford you buying power and the best way to obtain and maintain such a rating is to live beneath your means. When I was employed in the world system, I appeared to live above my means. That's because I faithfully tithe 10% or more off the gross of all my income and am a generous and sacrificial giver to the work of the Lord. When you precede the payment of your monthly bills in such a way you will see your finances multiply beyond that which people can figure from what they can see with the natural eye.

Some people think living on a budget binds or restricts you. How absurd! Only those not on a budget or not administering it properly think in such a way. On the contrary, a good budget gives you maximum flexibility and makes the best use of your dollars to stretch them further. Of course, when you first go on a budget, if you are now a frivolous spender you will experience a need to be self-disciplined for your old nature will not just go away without some resistance to the new determination for accountability. So, when you first start a budget, be mentally prepared to make some major adjustments to make the net income you actually have on hand meet all the obligations you must pay on a monthly basis. In plain English, if, once you've listed your total monthly net income and your total monthly obligations, you find that you bring in much less money than the monthly debt you have amassed you MUST get rid of something you are currently paying on and keep reducing your material possessions until your monthly net income becomes greater than your monthly obligations.

Your debt management may be so much out of control that even after you've done this "cutting away" you may have to go on an "Interim Budget" for a few months, first, before you can live on your "Ideal Budget". An Interim Budget does not list any "nice to have frills" an Ideal Budget does. These two types of budgets are addressed thoroughly in the next chapter, Planning Your Budget. To appreciate the value of the budget system, you must read that chapter.

When I've invested large sums of money in God's ministry work, the funds are always generated from assets derived from my long-term commitment to sticking to a budget system. Following the guidance in the next chapter, Chapter 12, is your start toward financial freedom in just a few years. Before going to Chapter 12, you need to commit to live by the following:

1.   **Develop sales resistance.**   Tupperware? Door-to-door sales? A new dress on sale (75% off)? Saying "no" costs you nothing.

2.   **Lead a more moderate lifestyle in all areas.** If you wear brand names, your children will too. If you swoon over a Mercedes, they will too.

3. Don't react to circumstances but follow your budget plan. A circumstance is something that arises from nowhere, it seems; yet, it happens at a time that causes us to shift things around in our budget if we are to respond to it. A circumstance seems as though it is an emergency when it occurs; however, it is just a mere situational inconvenience which we should respond to with the least amount of resources expended so that we may continue following the budget plan we have established. When a circumstance arises, we will soon discover what type of individual we are: reactive or proactive. A reactive person will respond to a circumstance in a way that will exhaust budget funds when no monies were alloted to deal with such a circumstance suddenly occurring. A proactive person will review his budget and either ignore the circumstance or deal with it with little or no tampering with budgeted expenses.

If you get a flat tire and it's not in the budget, get a $15 used tire until the car repair/maintenance "pocket" of your budget has sufficiently grown. For a couple of years I dressed my car with a set of $80, balanced, used tires to keep in line with my budget. Just 6 months ago I had a blow out on a steel-belted radial which I had purchased new just 9 months before but because I had traveled over 31,000 miles since I had purchased it there was no trade-in value. So, I purchased a $15 balanced, used tire and 6 months (and almost 20,000 miles) later, I replaced that used tire with a new one. Why did I wait so long? It was in good condition (I kept my eye on it.) and God kept it until I had the money in my budget.

"...I have led you forty years in the wilderness: your clothes are are not waxen old upon you, and thy shoe is not waxen old upon upon thy feet." (Deu 29:5)

It is very important for you to understand that all of the circumstances that present themselves to you do not accidentally occur. Sometimes Satan sets up circumstantial decoys to throw you off your budget. How you respond to this set-up will determine whether he'll present another situation or not. If you fall prey to the trap, he will continue to present circumstance after circumstance after circumstance until you're just steps short of a financial crisis. If you discover that such a pattern is occurring in your budget, you must immediately stop, re-focus your energies toward God's biblical road-map for your money and in some cases let the circumstance that has surfaced just sit without pouring another penny down that financial "invisible hole". You will find such "invisible holes" existing behind many car repairs, car purchases, fast cash loans, and door-to-door sales to name a few. If you have not yet read chapters 1 and 4, now is a great time to stop and do so to gain more revelation knowledge on evil spiritual entrappings which are nothing but financial vacuums that will suck every ounce of air out of your budget, your time with the Lord, your family life, and even your marriage.

4. Live beneath your means. Don't spend more than you make and don't spend all that you make.

5. Maintain a good credit history. Because history does repeat itself, your past credit record will have an impact on your present and future spending habits.

6. Avoid charge cards. When I discovered that I was charging our card to the max yet paying it off every year, I stopped to consider my ways. When I paid it off the next year, I cut it up because I really didn't need it. Since then, I've enjoyed the freedom of living on cash. I could not go back to the credit card for when I sought God's counsel He plainly spoke to me through Isaiah 30:1-3 that a credit card is a covering from the world system and He is a covering; we could not have it both ways. Seek God's counsel about the use of credit card(s). Then if you know God has released you to use one, get one that requires monthly pay-offs on the accrued balance (no interest) and which has no annual fees. Also adjust the credit limit to your personal buying power.

7. When you run into a financial tight spot, prioritize which bills to put on hold for that month. When something comes up you've not sufficiently prepared for (i.e. a blowout) you may have to place a bill on hold this month and catch up the next. You can make that juggling with your utility bills. They are usually amiable about making adjustments to the due date and they don't blemish your credit history. It is important to call first to make the necessary arrangements. I told one lady this and she tried it the next time she fell short in her budget. However, the utility she chose to place on hold did not work with her. I had forgotten to tell her to pray, before even making the call, that God might give her favor with the representative helping her. (Prayer does change things.)

It's important to comment here on your stewardship of your utilities. If you are constantly late paying your utilities or have high utilities because of a wasteful lifestyle, don't look for any utility to work with you on paying your bill late, even for one week. Utilities are there to make your home livable, not a place of slothfulness. Wasteful use of your utilities includes lengthy and multiple long distance phone calls, letting electricity run in rooms needlessly and using water excessively when you could have gotten the job done with much less water.

If your dollar needs are greater than your utility bill would be, consider borrowing from a relative who won't charge you any interest and may even set up a payment schedule that fits your individual financial handicap (i.e. repayment at tax refund time, repayment with a combination of money and work around their home or custodial work in their business in the evenings.). You may be surprised at how God could use your skills to bless someone else's plumbing, wallpapering, carpentry, or electrical needs. They may have what you need and you may have what they need.

8. Learn how to cut corners. Go manual and do it yourself. When you learn how to cut corners you will do wonders with pennies:

-I've made curtains, even with swags and cascades, with just a prayer and a picture from the catalog.

-God gave me the wisdom to upholster a chair and three sofas, without training but with just a prayer, a staple gun and some wholesale material.

-He led me as I wallpapered many rooms.

-I've made many bedspreads with pillows shams and bedruffles, without a pattern.

-The Lord gave me the wisdom to make cloth napkins out of scrap material. Later, when paper napkins ran out just days before my budget was scheduled to replenish the grocery list, we had napkins we could set up in the style of a fan on each plate with a candle lit while we ate! My children loved times like these.

-When we had no envelopes, I made some from typing paper and scotch tape.

-When condiments ran out, we turned the bottles upside down to get it all. (We paid for it all, didn't we?)

-We also made beautiful creative birthday cards from scrap paper and poster board.

- We saved pretty bags from store shopping to use as gift wrapping paper. Even your newspaper comic strips make colorful wrappers. The homemade curly bows we made for the box tops were just envied by so many inquisitive people.

-When your child needs a costume or piece of apparel on a one day's notice, get a simple pattern and make it. My daughter waited until the last minute to tell me of a need for a dress. I made it that very night and she wore it the next day. It only took the time you'd spend watching a typical movie on TV.

9. Have household rules and stick with them. If you plan to successfully execute your budget, you must set household rules for everyone in the house to follow. The person who plans the budget is not the only one who uses the utilities and consume the food within the home; therefore, conservation must be practiced by all.

Rules are just guidelines that establish boundaries and boundaries are not all that confining. They shouldn't constrict but add a secure feeling. To a child, that's just what house rules represent, "feelers" which define, distinguishing between the permitted and the unpermitted. Kids don't mind rules which give them direction as to how far to go, if you begin such rule-setting early in life. It is when we let time slide that we then have to confront the wall of rebellion that we've allowed to build.

Involve your children in the rule-setting process. If you haven't lived by household rules before, don't bombard them with a wad of restrictions. Bring in a few guidelines at a time 'til you've covered all areas you need to bring in line or want to see improvements in.

Ask them, "What would you suggest as a good time to turn the TV set off during weekdays? Weekends? What's a good day to fast from TV? How should we assign chores within the house outside the perimeters of your bedroom?...." Then, using their input, plan the house rules. Write them down and pass them out to the kids. Have periodic family meetings to follow up, compliment and make revisions as your children mature.

In enforcing the rules you expect your children to live by, it's very important that when other children come over to treat them the same as you would treat your own, that is, the same rules apply to all. For example, if when your child is picky about a meal you've prepared for him to eat and you make him eat it anyway or nothing at all, when a visiting child stays over long enough to have dinner with your family, you shouldn't stop in the middle of the meal to fix a "special" plate just because the child doesn't like what you've cooked. This move will help your children to have more respect for the household rules and feel "special" themselves.

You will find that, in time, your children will become self disciplined, serious managers of their time and resources. For a sample of the household rules I established to raise my children on, see the *Family Planner*, the companion workbook to this text. In it, you will see that as my own sisters and brothers stayed with us, they too had to fall in line with the household rules and energy conservation schedules. The *Family Planner* also has blank forms for use in planning your own household rules.

10. Learn how to swallow your American pride and live on the basics. A lot of resources are expended today on items which exonerate American Pride (the two-three car family, designer clothing and footwear promoting sports idols, etc.). Your children learn by what they see you do more than by what you say. Be content and they will be too.

Don't give your children everything you

can afford to buy them. Coming from a small rural town, I knew how having a little could allow your creative imagination to flow. When I was a teenager, I learned to sew and used my piano playing gift to play for several churches in the area. So, when my parents could not afford to give us everything we wanted, this didn't bother me. As a teenager, if I felt I still wanted an item, I'd either make it or work/played the piano to earn the money I needed and purchased it myself.

When my children wanted things they could not buy with their allowance money, I allowed them to work but only during the summer of their Junior and Senior high school years. Then, they could buy things they wanted that I thought were too extravagant, like an expensive pair of tennis shoes, a phone for their car, a stereo system for their bedrooms, or other frills. However, when they got paid they chose to do other-wise. The house rules, home budget plan, chore sched-ule, TV schedule, Bible studies, family coun-seling, family prayers, and other disciplines had finally paid off. They didn't desire to buy any of these things. Instead, during the summer months they paid their tithes, bought clothes on sale, helped me buy groceries, paid for their own gas, bought their dad a birthday gift on his summer birthday, and saved money whenever they weren't lending it to me. I learned through their frugality that the things I could afford to buy them but didn't, weren't that important to them after all.

11. Learn the difference between a conven-ience versus a necessity. A convenience allows you to get something accomplished with little effort on your part by simplifying your work and requiring less of your time. A necessity is something that's indis-pensable; a required need. It's a conven-ience to have a washing machine in your home. But it really isn't necessary. The necessity is to have clean clothes.

The same is true for a dryer, a variety of clothing and shoes, beauty parlor visits, etc.

12. Invest in others. Help others (your neighbor, the elderly, even your enemies to win them) when there's a need. We have done this so much that God blessed us when my children went off to college: The church came over and installed a garage door opener and outside security lights. The only cost was to purchase the material and host lunch for everyone.

13. Become a steward over the money you earn. Learn to mentally give everything back to God. You must give an account to Him of how you managed all funds, not just the 10% tithe but also of how you paid your bills and amassed debt. You must learn to transfer ownership that you may allow God to work supernaturally in your budget. Learn to pray about purchases before making them (Should I get it? Is this the one? Is this the proper time? Is this the right company to buy from?) Every decision in the use of your money should be based on Scriptural principles. See Appendix D for a discussion on various Scriptural principles which deal with your handling of God's finances. See Chapter 10, Trusting God To Meet Your Needs, for a more detailed discussion on stewardship versus ownership. Remember, your Heavenly Father provides for you and He wants you to be accountable for the funds He's entrusted you with.

14. Don't get caught naked! Stay Covered! The two "biggies" you should never tamper with are tithes (your spiritual covering) and your house/rent payment (your physical covering). You need your spiritual covering to come against attacks on your finances which you can not see with the natural eye. (Did you know your money can take on wings and fly away?) You need your physical covering to be a good provider for your family.

God is organized. He is a God of detailed planning. When you begin to see your budget as an organized way to track your accountability to God of how you've handled all the funds He's entrusted you with, you will appreciate the value of your budget plan.

Going to a budget system will make your entire family feel secure and they will become more responsible with finances themselves just from being around you, the family budget manager!

This section is an extract from *Raising Responsible Children In a Single Parent Home.*

If you are genuinely convenanting with the Lord to live by these 14 budget commitments, when you finish this chapter, find a quiet place where you can repeat these commitments to the Lord, alone, then give Him your signature as a sure sign.

____
signature

WHAT'S THE SCRIPTURAL BASIS OF A GOOD BUDGET?

Scripturally, you need to maintain a good budget to --

• Maintain accountability and faithfulness to God in your stewardship.

"If therefore ye have not been faithful in the unrighteous mammon, who will commit to your trust the true riches?" (Luke 16:11)

• Have a plan by which you may manage payments.

"(Sit)....down first and...(count) the cost whether (ye) have sufficient to finish ....." (Luke 14:28-30)

• Stay disciplined when you can't see progress because of spiritual hindrances.

"There is an evil which I have seen under the sun, and it is common among men: A man to whom God hath given riches, wealth, and honor, so that he wanteth nothing for his soul of all that he desireth, yet God giveth him not power to eat thereof, but a stranger eateth it: this is vanity, and it is an evil disease."
(Ecclesiastes 6:1-2)

"Wilt thou set thine eyes upon that which is not? for riches certainly make themselves wings: they fly away as an eagle toward heaven." *(Proverbs 23:5)*

ADVANTAGES OF A SOUND BUDGET

It's good planning to have a sound budget. The LORD believes in thorough plans. He knows that's the best way to see a project to its end. Remember these thorough plans God gave to His appointed leaders?

- The layout of the Tabernacle of the Congregation. (to Moses)
- The layout of the temple which Solomon would build. (to David)
- The high priest and priests robes and garments. (to Moses)
- The sacrificial offering types (to Moses)

SCRIPTURAL BASIS FOR BUDGET POCKETS

Budget Pockets are just banking accounts or home kept files we set up and maintain to let our funds sit for withdrawal either electronically or manually that we may more easily manage what we have on hand and where it goes when withdrawn.

Scriptural Basis --

Ecclesiastes 11:1-2

"Cast thy bread upon the waters: for thou shalt find it after many days. Give a portion to seven, and also to eight; for thou knowest not what evil shall be upon the earth." Ecclesiastes 11:1-2

Matthew 25:27

"Thou oughtest...to have put my money to the exchangers..." KJV

"...invested my money with the bankers..." Amplified

"...put my money in the bank..." New American Standard

"...put my money on deposit..." New International Version

FOR MEN ONLY: CAN I TRUST MY WIFE AS THE BUDGET KEEPER?

The Bible says, YES!!!

*"......I will make him an **help meet** for him....And the rib, which the LORD God had taken from man, made He a woman, and brought her unto the man...because she was taken out of Man."* *(Gen 2:18, 20-23)*

Strong's Concordance gives the following definition to the hebrew word, "ezer", from which the word "help meet" originates : aid, succour, help.

Today, both Webster's and World Book Encyclopedia dictionaries define Help-Meet as:
> ➡ Help-Mate   ➡ Wife

One who
- surrounds; succours; promotes
- changes for the better
- remedies; relieves; supports
- assists in time of want, need, danger, trouble, or distress

THE RULER AND THE LAWGIVER

The Bible bestows leadership roles, for the husband and wife, which are all derived from the husband's covering leadership:

"My son, hear the instruction of thy father, and forsake not the law of thy mother." (Prov 1:8)

"My son, keep thy father's commandment, and forsake not the law of thy mother." (Prov 6:20)

"She openeth her mouth with wisdom; and in her tongue is the law of kindness." (Prov 31:26)

"...the head of every man is Christ...of the woman is the man..... of Christ is God." (I Cor 11:3)

These Scriptures lay out before us all, God's orderly division of leadership between the husband and wife; thus, we find these family leadership principles in Scripture:
- The family's instruction comes from dad. (Prov 1:8)
- The family's law comes from mom. (Prov 1:8)

112

• The wife's law is founded on instruction received from the husband, whose instruction is founded on the Word of God. (I Cor 11:3)

• The family rule (commandment) comes from the husband. (Prov 6:20)

• The wife's role is to establish how that rule (commandment) will be applied. (law = application of rules. I Cor 11:3)

Rule from husband: *"We can't afford any steaks this week; my hours were cut back at work. This ($) is all we can spend on groceries this week."*

Law of wife applying that rule: She goes out, finds ground beef on sale; buys a big batch, and makes five delightfully different meals from it throughout the week: Golden Mushroom Meatloaf, Saucy Beef Mandarin, Ground Beef Casserole Bake, Meat Balls Italiano, and Juicy Cheesy Burgers. So, the LORD blessed the work of her hands.....

*"She considereth a field **(from among all the meats she spies the ground beef)**, and buyeth it **(and buys it)**: with the fruit of her hands **(working it with her hands)** she planteth a vineyard **(she produces a variety of ground beef dishes)**." (Prov 31:16)*
(**Bold** = my insertions)

FOR MEN ONLY:
THE QUALITIES OF A HELP-MEET

When you treat your wife as a "Help-Meet" rather than a dependent or a room-mate, you are going to see certain biblical truths take hold in the resources in your home:

Proverb 31

• Her financial wisdom will become priceless to your family's budget. (Prov 31:10)

• You'll begin to TRUST her God-given financial management skills. (vs 11)

• When you let the rich resources of the Help-Meet begin to reproduce through her, you and the children will praise her for how she has blessed the household because as a steward/bookkeeper, she will keep the books in the fear of the LORD, the true owner of all your family resources. (vs 28, 30)

• Her good financial resource management will speak for itself. (vs 31)

• You will then see that her divine calling from God must be fulfilled within the HOME. (vs 15, 21, 26, 27; Prov 6:20, II Tim 3:6)

• She will not become wasteful with the family resources. (vs 11)

• She'll make you look good in front of others. (vs12)

• She'll become a diligent, hard worker within the home, to the benefit of the entire household. (vs 13-15)

• She'll consider before she buys. "wise planning, wise purchases, cultivation of what she buys..." (vs 16-19)

• She'll remember the blessings of giving to the poor. (vs 20, Matt 25:34-40)

• Her thriftiness allows the family to dress as ROYALTY. (vs 22)

• After all, you'll be known in the city for your wealth and influence because of her application of sound biblical financial principles. (vs 23)

• Her hands are anointed to reproduce. (vs 22, 24, 25)

• Her mouth, is anointed with wisdom. (vs 26)

FOR MEN ONLY:
FINANCIAL GHOSTS FROM THE PAST

When you have unpaid debt from the past, especially that which you don't intend to pay, you have

unresolved spiritual sins which will hinder your current walk with the LORD and any current or future financially based dealings. Some of these debts are so old that they have been erased off the books of those individuals or businesses owed to, but not erased off Satan's books. Such debt include, but is not limited to:
- Unpaid Child Support
- Unpaid Child Birth Bills
- Unpaid College loans
- Unpaid Charge Cards

- Cash Debt Owed To An X-Friend (that's probably why they are X)

- Money Borrowed & "Slipped" from Parents

- Borrowed Car You Totalled 5 Years Ago, Unsettled

Some of these debts would also apply to women, as well. Regardless how much Christians tell you that *"Jesus' blood has washed away all your past sins. You don't have to go back and clear up anything"*, past financial sins require restitution. Zacchaeus restored fourfold (four times the original amount) for false accusations (Luke 19:8-9). A false accusation could be anything from speaking in pretense, to cheating and deceiving. This attempt to restitute must be geniuine. It may draw a balanced due or a clear forgiveness; yet, this attempt to provide restitution must be made. See chapters 2 and 3 and Appendix C for further discussion on the handling of past debt.

THE MISCONCEPTION ABOUT
BUDGET PLANS

Many misconceive that a budget plan is for poor money managers who are consistently delinquent and in trouble. This is an obvious lie of Satan who wants you to be poor, delinquent, in trouble and too proud to correct these mistakes. Satan knows you're playing with God's money, not yours, and when you mismanage God's money, you're befriending Satan! A consistently delinquent person doesn't want to see his faults laid out before him. He's ashamed, which later leads to pride, when he continues to avoid honestly looking at his faults.

THE TRUTH ABOUT BUDGET PLANS

A budget is for a family who --
- Wants to be organized.
- Wants to know where their money goes.
- Wants to drive at night with their headlights on.
- Wants to be accountable to God for their stewardship.
- Sees a roadmap:
    - A way of arriving at their destination = *financial freedom*
    - At the earliest time = *early payoff*
    - Using the least amount of gas = *least $*
    - With the least amount of wear & tear = *least amount of ignorant decisions, $ sins, $ curses, and repeatedly starting over & over again*
    - On their automobile = *their means of making money*

CHAPTER 12

PLANNING YOUR BUDGET

INCOME

Before beginning, let's distinguish between your "usable income" and "net income". Your usable income consists of -

(a) all net pay from your employment,
(b) retirement pay,
(c) overtime pay,
(d) child support, and
(e) funds generated from doing odd jobs for short periods of time.

(Note: You should also include interest payments received from your savings, certificates of deposit, mutual funds and other investments but these aren't usually liquidated by the consumer on a monthly basis.)

Your net income consists of the money that's paid to you by your employer after all taxes, insurances, pensions, and other company deductions have been made from your salary, this includes all jobs you regularly work. You will use this figure to plan your budget because you can depend on it. Income from c + d + e, above, may be periodic and may change in amounts received but don't use this as joy money! These funds should be used to help pay off and "close out" consumer debt and to beef up savings.

ESTABLISHING BUDGET POCKETS

When you receive your income, don't leave large sums of money laying around the house. Chances are you'll spend it on something else (i.e.

responding to a circumstance rather than following your budget plan.) A good budgeteer has monies in several different pockets; that's what the government does. Your pocket system should be comprised of banking institutions, your credit union, mutual funds\life insurance, your church and a small money file at home. Once dispersed you can set up electronic transfers for payroll deposits and automatic drafts for payment of some long term obligations (i.e. house payment, insurance, and some utilities). You need to set up these pockets so you won't spend a lot of time paying bills monthly. Many people pay financial managers large sums of money to pay their bills for them, relieving them of the stress. By setting up pockets you can let the banking institution and your credit union pay many of your bills automatically by setting up drafts.

From a $60,000 usable income base, after setting up the bank drafts, the residue of our paycheck, bi-weekly, was only $187. It didn't bother us because we knew the major bills (mortgage, college notes, insurances, piano, and some utilities) were being paid on time. The fees are small. It won't mess up as long as you just forget about the fact that the money exists and just plan the part of the budget you will be managing based on the net income you'll have left. That's the bottomline figure you'll have to work with. You should be writing only about 8 checks and maintaining a small cash file at home. Your pocket system will look something like the following budget disbursement diagram:

THE BUDGET POCKETS SYSTEM

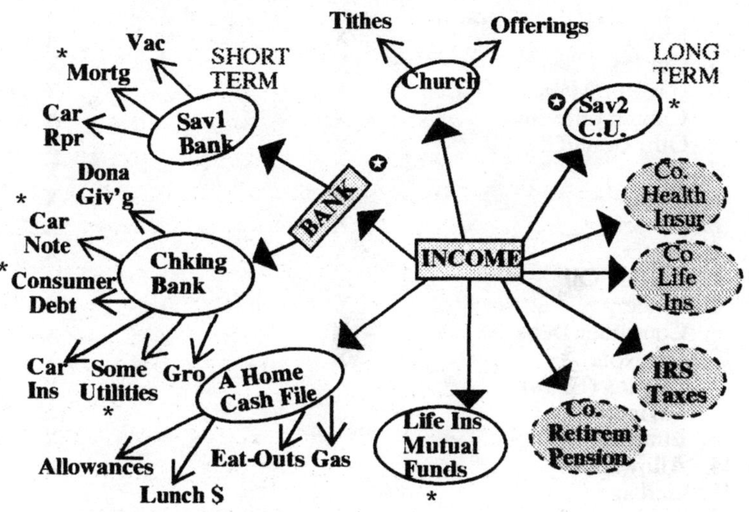

*   Automatic Drafts
⬯   Pockets you place your net income in for distrib, investm't, etc.
⬭   Pockets which are mandatory deductions from your gross income
✪   Payroll Deposits
C.U. Credit union

INTERIM vs IDEAL BUDGET PLAN

An Interim Budget does not list any "nice to have frills"; an Ideal Budget does. You must determine which budget plan to use: Interim or Ideal.

Notice that the bills/obligations in the next chart are prioritized from MOST to LEAST important. You must approach your budget in this way or else when tight times come you may not think and cut something of higher importance (i.e. tithes) while paying something of less importance (i.e. cable, garbage collection, eat-out, etc.). An Ideal Budget is designed to make you not feel penalized for having debt. So you have debt. Now work your way out of it, but slowly, just as you slowly crept into it.

		INTERIM BUDGET	IDEAL BUDGET
1.	Tithes	X	X
2.	Mortg	X	X
3.	Car Ins	X	X
4.	Car Rpr/Maint	X	X
5.	Church Offerings	X	X
6.	Othr Dona/Giv	X	X
7.	Gas	X	X
8.	Phone	X	X
8.	Electric	X	X
8.	Water	X	X
8.	Heating Oil	X	X
8.	Grocery	X	X
9.	Consumer Debt	X	X
10.	Car Note	X	X
11.	Life Ins (Extra)		X
12.	Savings		X
13.	Lunch $		X
14.	Allowances		X
15.	Garbage		X
16.	Cable		X
17.	Eat-Out		X
18.	Vacation		X

If you feel you need to go on an interim budget first, remember, your goal is to pay-off obligations (i.e. consumer debt/car note) which you will closeout before going on your Ideal Budget as you determine to lead a more modest lifestyle.

Now, with a pen and paper at hand, let's determine the best plan for you:

1. List all of your net income.

2. List all of your financial obligations and debts.

3. Subtract No. 2 from No.1 This is what you have left over to save, vacation with, eat out on, etc.

4. If your answer to No. 3 was 0 or a minus, you need to plan an Interim Budget to get rid of the excess debt. If you had a major credit (i.e. $300) you can

proceed to Step 5, Your Ideal Budget. If not, you need to plan your Interim Budget at this time.

Interim Budget. Remember that your interim budget is temporary. It is designed to give you time to pay off certain consumer debt and possibly your car note before advancing to an ideal budget. If your debt ratio is high you'll need to liquidate those possessions we talked about in Chapter 11 to generate start-up funds to totally pay off (without reopening later) consumer debt first, then deal with your car note. Many people who have readjusted their budget for one reason or another (from taking the wife out of the workforce to starting an entrepreneurship) have started with the car, the main dollar eater. If you have two or more cars, you have the option of selling all but one. (Even if you are a couple and both of you work, you can work out a travel schedule. It's just a temporary inconvenience that will get finances back in order.) If you have a new or late model car, you have the option of selling it and purchasing a well kept older model. This will also lower your car insurance and personal property tax. Also, you will be surprised to know that an older car doesn't necessarily increase your car repair\maintenance bill. (See item 4. under the Ideal Budget). You should not stay on the interim budget for more than a year. If after that time you still have a balance on your consumer debt/car note, ask your banker to roll it into a consolidation loan and have them draft it directly from the savings/checking pocket you've set up. This is a one time consolidation that should not be done again.

Ideal Budget. Now that you are ready to plan your ideal budget you can set up your bank drafts, if you haven't already done so. You can now readjust the net income figure you'll be working with at home to pay those bills you will be personally responsible for mailing checks to. Your ideal budget plan will be larger than your interim budget plan but because of the automatic drafts you've set up, you can just write "auto draft" across many of these obligations and concentrate on those you have to pay directly to the creditor or recipient yourself. Here's some guidance on dealing with each of these individual obligations/bills.

      1. TITHES. Faithfully pay your tithes and offerings. Pay your tithes out of obedience and give generous and sacrificial offerings out of faith that God will supply your needs. This is where the blessings will come from in your money's ability to stretch. Your tithes should be based on all of your USABLE INCOME, thus the exact amount may change from month to month. But if all of your extra income is cut off, you will always have your permanent income from your job(s) to tithe on; therefore, your tithes will never fall below 10% of your GROSS income from your job(s). See Chapter 4 for more on tithing.

Tithing on Increase. At times, you will receive certain increase in income that is titheable. Yet, all increase is not true increase, thus, is not titheable.

Some examples of funds you may receive that are not true increases are:

- Rent monies you receive from your adult children or siblings when you've set that rent at a rate that equals to what utility or grocery increase he has incurred.
- Your income tax refund check, if you paid tithes throughout the year on the gross of your income.
- Insurance reimbursement on an automobile loss when the reimbursement check was equal to or less than what you paid for the automobile (if you were paying tithes

as you were paying for this vehicle.)

Some examples of funds you may receive that ARE true increases on which you MUST pay tithes are:

- Rent monies you receive from boarders which you've set at a flat rate, monthly, above what the boarder has consumed.
- Income tax refunds based on your EARNED INCOME CREDIT. Money you receive back above what you have actually put in is EXTRA money.
- Insurance reimbursements of any kind that are above what you have put in.

2. MORTGAGE/RENT. Always look to spend the least amount on interest and insurance when you buy a home. Set up your mortgage payments to be automatically drafted from your bank account. If you already own a home, you should also situate yourself to take advantage of interest and insurance breaks; the key is that you maintain a good payment history on your mortgage.

From 30 to 15 Year Mortgage. After you've trimmed your bills and have been on your ideal budget for a while think about reducing your 30 year mortgage to a 15 year one. You're trimming away years of interest payments and you'll pay off your home, your largest long-term bill, and become financially independent sooner!

Private Mortgage Insurance (PMI). Most people don't know that you don't have to keep paying PMI for the life of your mortgage. You personally get no benefit from it; The insurance that you benefit from include homeowners (covers replacement cost, if destroyed by fire, etc.) and any mortgage insurance you purchase, separate from the mortgage, to pay off the balance should death occur. When we learned that the PMI could be removed after three years, we requested it and it was removed. Our monthly house payment of $877.94 was immediately reduced by $26.92. That's a savings of $323.04 a year! That's a nice amount of extra money.

Bi-weekly Plan. Just as soon as you get your automatic draft set up, consult with your mortgage company about getting on the bi-weekly plan. The bi-weekly plan allows you to pay the same amount you are already paying monthly on your home, except you pay exactly half this normal monthly payment, every 14 days. Paying this way results in two extra bi-weekly payments per year and these are applied directly to your principle, cutting about three years off your mortgage payoff date. Switching to the bi-weekly plan reduced our 20 year mortgage note by $14,069.53 and reduced the payoff date to 17 years; yet, the amount of our monthly house note remained the same! The bi-weekly plan also builds up equity faster. We recently relocated to another State and upon selling our home, after eleven years there, our cash position was greatly enhanced. By starting with a 20 year mortgage, removing the PMI after 3 years, and staying on the bi-weekly plan, we reaped over $50,000 in this sale. This house was originally purchased for $80,000.

3. CAR INSURANCE. Just make sure you're paying the cheapest rates for coverage needed.

4. CAR REPAIR/MAINTENANCE. My only advice here is to keep your car up. With an older model car, buy rebuilt parts from a discount auto parts store. You may think, "I only use new parts in my car." Use reason: if your car is old, you don't always need new parts. In fact, many times new parts will cause you to have problems with other old parts, sooner. You're probably thinking that if you traded

your newer car for an earlier model your repair bills will be very expensive. As I stated in our discussion of the interim budget, you will be surprised to know that an older car doesn't necessarily increase your car repair bill. This is 1998. In 1987, we bought a new van valued at $21,000. We spent roughly $450 a year in maintenance bills and our monthly payments on it were $355 a month. In 1991, while still paying on it, it was totaled in an accident. We used part of the insurance proceeds to purchase two immaculately kept older model cars, both 1984's, one for myself and the other for the children. The car purchased for me (at $2,400) had 84,000 miles on it. Seven years later it's still in great driving condition. Six months ago, the annual maintenance bill totaled about $700, the cost of two monthly payments on our van, ten years ago. I say six months ago because the LORD prompted me to bless a lady and her family with this dependable car last year for they had gone months without transportation due to a car loss with no money to replace it. (We had named the car 'Ole Glory when I drove it. It gives my heart great joy to see 'Ole Glory in the Church parking lot each Sunday as we drive up, for she now serves someone else whom God sees fit to bless.) 'Ole Glory, a Chevrolet, registered 258,000 miles six months ago and today she registers over 265,000. (This is the miracle car in chapters 4 and 15.) The key is to change your oil every month and to buy the car from a person who kept the maintenance up. Ask for papers on it. (Additionally, we cut our car payment bill to zero, car insurance premium down to a modest amount, and property tax bill down to a token amount.) That's your answer to the question: Aren't old cars unreliable? You've got to be motivated to downgrade your lifestyle from a late model car to an older model. Our motivation: to have the money to send the children to college. Your motivation: to balance your budget.

5. CHURCH OFFERINGS. This area is covered sufficiently under *Tithes and Offerings* in Chapter 4, Financial Curses. Learn what true sacrificial giving is in Chapter 8, Learning to Give.

6. OTHER DONATIONS AND GIVING. Charity and concern for our brethren in distant areas is endorsed by God (Acts 11:29-30). Many churches aren't obeying this Scripture today in support of such "lone" ministries but there is no reason why we shouldn't pick up the slack for there's a blessing out there for those who do. My family has been blessed for blessing others through giving beyond offerings to our local church to the giving of generous and sacrificial offerings to several distant evangelistic ministries. Your giving is not limited to money. It includes items you've been hoarding and those stored away for a garage sale. The Bible didn't say, 'sell and it shall be given unto you'. It says, *"Give and it shall be given unto you."* When you do give, do it joyfully with a free and willing heart.

7. GAS. Try to get everything done while you are out because many parents put 50+ miles on their car, after work, driving their children around in circles back and forth to after school and social events. Consolidating the trips and trading off days with other parents will reduce your gas bill.

8. UTILITIES and GROCERIES. Notice that your utilities and groceries are lumped together under one priority on the budget chart. That's because you can control the balance on these items. Your utilities and groceries will be as high or as low as you make them. Most people are very wasteful in these areas. You will have to really manage the household here. Appendix B gives you some charts which I actually

used to assign everybody's duties and run a smooth operation within the house. Some tips:

a. Electricity. Put energy saver devices on your hot water heater and air conditioner (AC) to turn them off when not needed. Monitor the big energy eaters: your oven, range, dryer, AC and hot water heater. Teach the children to use the microwave, toaster griddle, or some other small appliance to heat up food. Other energy saving tips can be found in Appendix B. (Note: This is a good place to mention that when we added attractive, inexpensive cloth awnings to the front and side windows it cut the summer temperature in the house down by 15 degrees, which also cut AC and attic fan use.)

b. Heating Oil. We heated our home and the water with heating oil. Now, you may think this next statement is cruel but <u>we slept with no heat in the winter.</u> We'd turn the thermostat to 65° after we got home from work/school and "off" when we went to bed. Many times in the dead of winter we'd heat the house with the Fireplace Insert. The kids were so healthy from the cool sleep that they had perfect attendance throughout high school. Even in their elementary years, James Jr. only missed one day in the sixth grade and Gala, three days in the first through third grades. They didn't have colds for we prayed when the symptoms came and the cold couldn't manifest itself. Also, the closed pores which hit the early morning winter chills guarded against winter colds attacks. A lady recently informed me that after she had finished reading my first book, *Raising Responsible Children,* she started turning the heat off at night on her asthmatic daughter who wheezes throughout the night. She said, from the very first night, her daughter started sleeping soundly, without the usual restlessness she was accustomed to having.

c. Water. Just tighten up on water waste. (i.e. letting the water run while you brush your teeth, letting the shower water run a lengthy time while you sing your favorite songs, flushing the commode multiple times, letting the kitchen sink water run while you wash and rinse dishes instead of using the sprayer gun, etc.) <u>On hot water heating:</u> When you think about the concept of heating water you can see that it's very wasteful. While nobody's home during the day (if you work) and while everyone's sleep at night, the hot water heater heats the water about every 45 minutes, that's thirty-two times a day! That's energy that no one is using yet, every month, you've got to pay for it. In fact, when you start turning the hot water heater "off", you will discover that most of your hot water bill is for the multiple times of re-heating when no one was home or using it because your bill will drop tremendously. What a waste!

d. Telephone. Check the telephone company services you have on your phone (i.e. call waiting, call forwarding, redialing, wire maintenance, return call, 3 way calling, caller ID, etc.) and determine if you've been using them enough to warrant the payments you make on these services. Also keep long distance calls short and to a minimum. Everything we think is an emergency really isn't. Some things can wait 'til we see the person. (Whatever happened to letter writing?) If you are experiencing long-distance abuse by a family member and have not seen a change in their behavior, put a block on your phone or install a payphone. Finally, consider using a discount telephone company instead of the big three: AT&T, MCI, & Sprint.

e. Groceries. When you buy with coupons (especially double coupon redemption), you can really save money. Many times when a one-time, small unexpected expense would appear I could pinch money off the groceries and never miss it for God seemed to bless such a wise move as I would bring in the same number of bags as I usually did! He saw that buying generic brands and dented cans (Check them first for leakage!) at such times was a great move. Many times children waste food because it's available (i.e. opening 3 boxes of cereal which all go stale at the same time). To stop this free run of the kitchen you can:

-- only allow them to go into one cabinet door. Put all the food for the school week in that cabinet. Transfer food from the other cabinets to there at the end of the week.

-- make the freezer off limits to all but yourself. Any freezer items which need to be moved to the refrigerator for their open indulgence should be moved there by you.

Sometimes before payday we were just down to wieners and bologna. That can put a damper on your family's spirit; so, to switch things around, after payday when our budget allowed us to replenish the groceries, I'd prepare the less costly meals first and as the weeks wore on and the less costly meals had been eaten, I pulled out the more costly meats and entrees. (Note: I speak in terms of weeks because I bought the main groceries once a month. I only "replenished" consumed items on a weekly basis.)

9. CONSUMER DEBT. Try to keep this short-termed: 90 days same as cash (no interest) and layaway. The only time you should get involved with a "Buy now and no payment/interest 'til next year" is when it overlaps your tax refund time. Then pay it off in full before the due date. If the item is so expensive that you can not pay for the entire indebtedness with your refund then you probably don't need the item. Consumer debt can be a growing albatross around your

neck, especially those with department stores, bank charge cards, and high-interest loan companies. Consumer debt will c-o-n-s-u-m-e you if you let it. That's why I recommend that you wipe this item off your budget as soon as possible.

10. CAR NOTE. When you're trying to balance an out of balance budget, you don't need a car note. It has been statistically proven that in a 30 year period of time, we spend more money on our cars than on our homes; see the analysis in chapter 13. Also, read the section on CAR REPAIR/MAINTENANCE, earlier in this chapter, for further discussion on your car needs.

11. EXTRA LIFE INSURANCE. Your job carries life insurance on you called "group policies". That's fine as long as you continue to work there. Most people have an additional policy on the side. Just make sure that you pick a reputable company and that you only take out a moderate amount.

12. SAVINGS. Actually, you'll need two savings accounts: a short term and a long term account. (See the budget pockets chart.) Your short term account is really your emergency funds for unforeseen expenses (i.e. household repairs, birthday/holiday gifts and taxes). You can also house your car repair/mainte-nance funds and vacation funds here. Your long term savings account should hardly ever be touched.

13. LUNCH. When your budget is tight, you can always fix your family boxed lunches from home.

14. ALLOWANCES. This is one area of responsibility that many of us will not grant to our children, only to the husband and wife, yet we don't understand why the children aren't good money managers when they grow up. Give them a small allowance but with discretion. You should hold their lunch and allowance money and give it to them on a

weekly basis. Purchase them an accordion-like letter-sized file with the compartments labeled: Lunch, Allowance and Tithes (this will come from their allowances.). This organized system will help them conserve money wisely. Responsibility breeds accountability.

15. GARBAGE COLLECTION. You really don't need it. It's just another frill. We carried our garbage to the county dump, bi-weekly. We paid $3 per visit which totaled $78 per year for 26 trips to the dump. When we had home collection services, we were paying $54 a quarter -- that's $216 a year!

16. CABLE. A cable bill can be high and is just an extension of television privileges. See my first book, *Raising Responsible Children*, for more on television privileges.

17. EAT OUTs. The family should eat out once in a while. It's refreshing for mom and dad and makes the children feel important. Just use moderation in selecting the places to eat. The cost must be within your budget limits.

18. VACATIONS. Everybody needs a break at least once a year. Sometimes we need it more often than that. Better yet, parents need a short honeymooner away from the children at least twice, annually. A vacation together, regardless how modest it may be, will do wonders in communications within the family. I'm not talking about a trip to grandma's house or to an 'ole high-school chum of yours but a fun, historical, educational trip to the national zoo (free!), Smithsonian Institute (free!), Disney World, the mountains, state parks (inexpensive) or some other get-away from the things you are accustomed to. It's worth saving for!

PERIODIC EXPENSES. You will have periodic expenses which aren't covered in your budget (school supplies, clothing, shoes, hair care, and lawn care, to name a few). To cut back on expenses, you can pull out the sewing machine for some clothing. You can fix your daughter's hair and cut your son's. Your entire family can take care of the lawn. School supplies are minimal and can be paid for with funds generated from those odds-and-ends jobs during the summer, prior to school.

NOW PLAN YOUR OWN BUDGET

After reading this chapter you should now be ready to plan your own budget. You will find worksheets in *Family Planner*, the companion workbook to this text. A handy pocket-sized quad-foldable grocery checklist is also provided in that workbook for your use.   Happy Budgeting!

*This chapter is an extract from *Raising Responsible Children In a Single Parent Home.*

CHAPTER 13

LIVING WITH YOUR BUDGET

BUDGET SCENARIOS

After studying the vices that come along with spending money and acquiring material possessions without considering the statutes of God, we are so terribly humbled. We then realize that our reverence of God is incomplete until He is reverently honored in the secret place of our purses and wallets. But oh, what healing oil the Holy Spirit brings when we sacrificially lay open the sinned-stained crevices of these walled, unholy sanctuaries of idolatry that He may wash away the many financial sins, curses and ignorances and then replace them with wisdom that can only be sent from heaven for who else would know our individual problematic situations but He.

Once we've studied and understood what it means to commit a financial sin or ignorance or to be under a financial curse, we can identify certain scenarios to stay away from when planning and executing our budgets. With this thought in mind, let's look at some scenarios to determine if these people are operating under a balanced budget, a budget that's catered to the flesh, or a cursed budget.

All three scenarios are planned for an unmarried individual bringing home a net monthly pay of $1,700. They all make $24,000 annually, get paid once monthly and own a 1989 car which is already paid off. Yet, they all lead different lifestyles. Budget Scenario - I is balanced, Scenario - II is geared to fleshly indulgences, and Scenario - III is plagued with curses. Study each one to see why.

BUDGET SCENARIO -- I (BALANCED BUDGET)

Annual-$24,000 MONTHLY	AMT DUE	BUDGET ITEM	1 JANUARY	1 FEBRUARY	1 MARCH
GROSS 2,000	$200	Tithe			
NET 1,700	450	Rent			
Paid 1st of mo	50	Car Ins			
Single Person	10	Car Maint			
'89 Car Paid Off	50	Church Ofgs			
	60	Gas			
	45	Phone			
	85	Electricity			
	35	Water			
	100	Groceries			
	270	Savings			
	0	Lunch			
	20	Allowances			
	30	Cable			
	20	Eat-Out			
Bal Due		**CONSUMER DEBT**			
$550	50	Furniture			
175	25	Charge Card #1			
	0	Charge Card #2			
	0	Charge Card #3			
3,200	100	Loan #1 (college)			
	0	Loan #2			
		PERIODIC DEBT			
from Sav'gs		Property Tax			
	100	Church Bldg Fund Pldg			
	1,700				

The individual in Budget Scenario I leads a modest lifestyle, doesn't overspend in any one area, gives generously and is saving for the future. His budget is BALANCED.

BUDGET SCENARIO -- II (FLESH ORIENTED BUDGET)

Annual-$24,000 MONTHLY GROSS 2,000 NET 1,700 Paid 1st of mo Single Person '89 Car Paid Off	AMT DUE	BUDGET ITEM	1 JANUARY	1 FEBRUARY	1 MARCH
	$200	Tithe			
	450	Rent			
	150	Car Ins			
	10	Car Maint			
	25	Church Ofgs			
	120	Gas			
	145	Phone			
	85	Electricity			
	75	Water			
	250	Groceries			
	0	Savings			
	0	Lunch			
	100	Allowances			
	30	Cable			
	60	Eat-Out			
Bal Due		**CONSUMER DEBT**			
		Furniture			
		Charge Card #1			
		Charge Card #2			
		Charge Card #3			
		Loan #1 (college)			
		Loan #2			
		PERIODIC DEBT			
$79	ovrdue	Property Tax			
$1,200	ovrdue	Chur Bldg Pldg (pd $300)			
	1,700				

BUDGET SCENARIO -- III (CURSED BUDGET)

Annual-$24,000 MONTHLY	AMT DUE	BUDGET ITEM	1 JANUARY	1 FEBRUARY	1 MARCH
GROSS 2,000		$200 Tithe			
NET 1,700	450	Rent			
Paid 1st of mo	50	Car Ins			
Single Person	10	Car Maint			
'89 Car Paid Off	50	Church Ofgs			
Balances Due	60	Gas			
overdue, $90	45	Phone			
overdue, $115	85	Electricity			
	35	Water			
	80	Groceries			
	0	Savings			
	0	Lunch			
	0	Allowances			
	30	Cable			
	0	Eat-Out			
		CONSUMER DEBT			
3,500	100	Furniture			
ovrdue,90; 4,350	90	Charge Card #1			
7,650	140	Charge Card #2			
8,750	150	Charge Card #3			
ovrdue,300; 9,500	150	Loan #1 (college)			
ovrdue,200; 5,006	200	Loan #2			
		PERIODIC DEBT			
ovrdue, $79	ovrdue	Property Tax			
ovrdue, 1,000	ovrdue	Church Bldg Fund Pldg			
	1,925				

HOUSE/CAR ANALYSIS

When studying the interest percentage chart in Chapter 1 you can see that the LORD gives us so much more in return for investing in His kingdom work than the world system gives us for investing in its investments; yet, we still continue to do it backwards. The best example of our dumping of large sums of cash into the world's method of "buying to own" is the way we let the purchase of automobiles hinder us from paying off a home within 15 years. Why are we comparing car purchases to home purchases here? Because over a 30 year period of time, we would have actually put as much money in our automobile purchases as we would have our home; yet, at the end of that period, the automobiles would just be a worthless heap of metal while the home would have doubled or more in value. (See Chapter 12 for the most preferred method in buying your home and getting into a pattern of spending less money on home and car interest combined.)

HOUSE/CAR ANALYSIS

Car Can Be Highest Ticket Item, Your Lifetime!!!

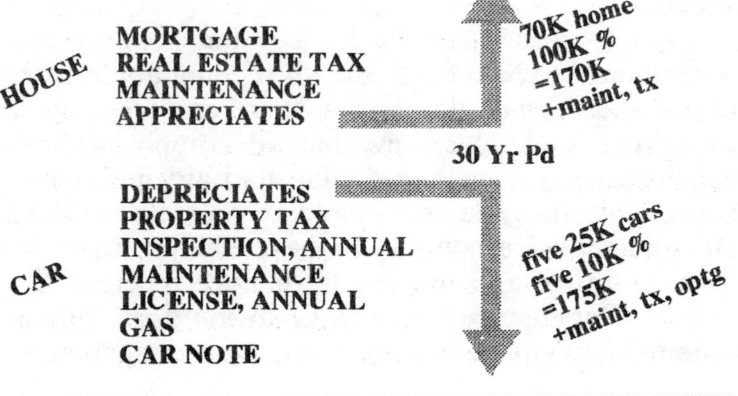

Since the lack of communication has always been an age-old problem, it would be an excellent move, on your part, to initiate contact with the lender on debt that needs refinancing or revision to come in line with major changes in your budget. They will work with you, if you let them know. But you must let them know or else it will appear as though you are evading them. They may be a secular business but God has their heart right in the palm of His hand, *"The king's heart is in the hand of the LORD, as the rivers of water: He turneth it whithersoever He will."* (Proverbs 21:1) See Chapter 3, for further discussions on using communication doorways.

SETTLING COURT-ORDERED
FINANCIAL JUDGEMENTS

A Judgement is a formal decision given by a court as a final order in a civil proceeding which leaves you with an amount of money to pay to settle a financial claim against you. After rendering the verdict, the judge signs a document called the Judgement or Decree of the court. This Judgement document must be honored by the person who owes said debt.

God has set such secular court room proceedings in place for those who do not abide by His ordained law; thus, decrees must be enforced, by the law of the land, to ensure that all comply with fair business dealings. If you have had any judgements against you and you've ignored paying all or part of that adjudicated amount, you have sinned, even if it was a long time ago and you have since repented from all sins. (Repentance is a change in mind and action.) Sometimes court judgements are waged against persons before salvation and sometimes after salvation. In any event, you are accountable to God for resolving such financial breaches even if they are so old (5 years, etc) that the people no longer harass you. Many Christians commit financial sins and see themselves as being persecuted or going through tests and trials when people of the world system come against them legally for not honoring debt owed to them. Yet, God's Word clearly shows that He has ordained the legal system as "ministers of God" to recognize good and punish evil committed by anyone who approaches their bench:

> *"Let every soul be subject to the higher powers. For there is no power but of God. Whosoever resisteth the power, resisteth the ordinance of God.....For he is the minister of God to thee to execute wrath upon him that doeth evil.....For this cause pay ye tribute also: for they are God's ministers, attending continually upon this very thing." (Romans 13:1-6)*

It is quite interesting to observe presumptuous Christians who see themselves as immune to the judicial system when it comes to worldly justice. They presume that God will overlook this breach of financial contract because of their holiness yet this is really "hole-liness" (the hole that the serpent comes through to bite us as we break the hedge of protection that God had given us prior to our willingness to overstep His defined boundaries which separate righteousness from sin--Eccles 10:8.) Because presumptuous sin is a natural violation of a spiritual law, it also gives evil spirits legal ground to execute God's temporal judgements of loss, tormenting trouble, failure, weaknesss, sickness, and even death to those who violate His laws (I Sam 16:14-16, I Cor 11:30, Hebrews 12:6-9).

What one fails to see is that many times there are financial failures in our past which leave open ground for Satan to have the legal right to send demonic leeches upon our current finances that seem to suck the blood out of every penny that comes through our hands -- that's all we see, "pennies going through our hands as we work, and pay, and nothing stays" (See Financial Holes, Chapter 1).

It is with this thought in mind that as I sat down with Allison (not her real name), a young lady who took this finance seminar, I pondered over the many unpaid judgements that she had not dealt with in over 5 years. I could not plan her current budget without considering these ghosts although she actually made enough money to take care of her current living expenses. I laid her budget needs before the Lord and during intercession He revealed to me that those judgements were the very reason for her not being able to get beyond living from pay-day to pay-day. She had given ground to Satan to operate against her finances because she had not honored financial pledges she had made to others in the past, with a promise to pay.

"Neither give place to the devil" Eph 4:27

People are destroyed because of the lack of knowledge (Hosea 4:6). Our ignorance is therefore providing Satan tremendous advantage to inflict us with demon spirits of financial consumption and with-holdings. When we have fulfilled the conditions which allow unclean demonic spirits to inflict shortages on our finances we have given them ground which can allow recurring short-comings which seem to bind up our ability to excel in the workforce:

-- only finding job openings in minimum wage opportunities.

-- always being the last hired and first fired.

-- finding, regardless what city or state we move to, all jobs we seem to get are just those where there's always someone who is an unfair boss, a prejudiced boss, an oppressing boss, etc.

-- finally, a job with educational benefits, yet,

we have a terrible accident on the job which causes us to have to curtail school just one semester shy of graduating and when our health is restored, the educational opportunity has ceased to be offered.

-- just, on and on suppressing and oppressing job conditions, just enough to live a basic lifestyle but never crawling out from under.

Considering Allison's situation and knowing the suggestion to her of getting in touch with these businesses could be opening a can of worms she may dread, I set to laying out an openly candid letter of acknowledgement of the debt and offering genuine repentive measures to restore within her financial means. Allison read these letters and mailed them like periodic time bombs. (See Appendix C for a sample letter should you need to do so.) She received no responses.

Now this may not seem like much of a surprise to you because most large businesses will write off small debt after several years. However, her own personal relief, physically, was evident in the peaceful glow on her face and, spiritually, this is the one most important fact you need to grasp: **Her contacting the businesses to ask forgiveness and offer terms of settlement closed the door on demon spirits to continue to hinder her financially. A physical gesture had to be initiated, on her part, to close a spiritual door she had left wide-open for several years. The ball was now in the businesses' court.**

If you find yourselves with unsettled financial ghosts from your past that you've forgotten about, you need to close these doors of legal ground through which Satan hinders your current and future financial capabilities. You may think you are doing alright, financially. But is this where you could be? Do you really make as much as you should, considering your education, hard work, and diligence? Are your siblings always doing better financially than you? Do you seem to always go to the Class Alumni Meeting with everyone doing better than you thought they would, but look at you? Do you find opportunities always slipping through your hands at the last minute with no logical explanation? (As you can see, these financial ghosts may have set a self-inflicted sin curse in motion on your budget.)

These are just a few words for thought, for where you can not logically figure out a reason for financial disparity, there is usually a spiritual reason and if one is there, Satan will block you from the opportunity to succeed when he sees you have ignored a wide open door of careless financial dealings.

Let's learn a lesson from Allison. Satan may want us to think we'll open a can of worms if we reach back into the past, but we'll actually be putting the smelly little critters back into their place, a sealed container.

"My transgression is sealed up in a bag, and thou sewest up mine iniquity." Job 14:17

COMING OUT OF
THE WILDERNESS

You are not meant to stay in the financial wilderness. It's not God's will, even if you wandered into there on your own through sins and error. The LORD expects you to learn that you are never without His undergirding when you have repented and turned toward Him in the way you manage His funds. The nickel in your pocket when you are broke? The prosperity anointing. But it only comes to those who do it God's way: plant what seed you have in Him; then, decrease that He may increase you, spiritually.

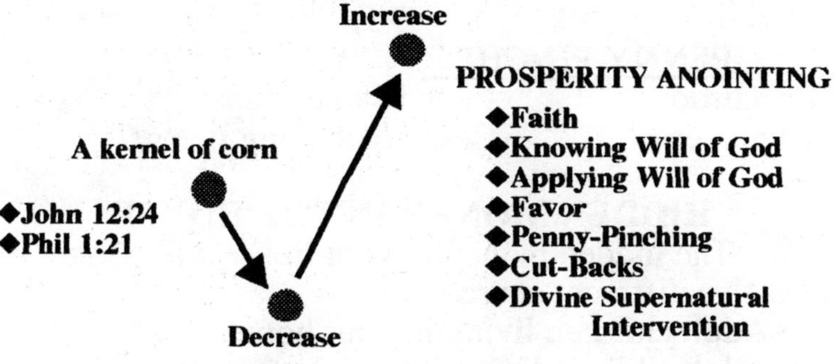

CUTBACKS AND PENNY PINCHING

Your cutbacks should be on items you consume for convenience and purchases you make based on the lust of the flesh, lust of the eye, and pride of life. Depending on the severity of your budget cramp, you will either have to reduce the amount you consume monthly (telephone budget reduced from $75 to $35, monthly) or sell and replace an item with one less expensive (i.e., to reduce a $500 car payment to a $250 car payment, monthly). When you decide which items you need to cut back on, be prepared to live with that change for an extended period of time (6 months, one year, etc.)

Your penny-pinching should hurt you, not your lenders. Penny-pinching is for a shorter period of time than cutbacks and may shift from one item to another, as necessary.

<u>CUTBACKS</u>
- Conveniences (cable, lunch, etc.)
- Utilities (garbage, telephone, water, electric, grocery, etc.)
- Consumer Debt (cards, loans, furniture,

clothing, etc.)
• Car Debt

<u>PENNY-PINCHING</u>
• hairdos   • long distance calls   • gas
• grocery   • flesh comforting items

HIDDEN MONEY IN THE HOUSE
The hidden money in your house will come
from five different sources:
• Adult children living in your home
• Adult siblings living in your home
• Adult relatives living in your home
• Sick persons living in your home

*"Nor did we eat any one's bread without paying for it, but with
toil and struggle we worked night and day, that we might not
be a burden or impose on any of you [for our support]....If any
one will not work, neither let him eat."*
II Thessalonians 3:8-10   (Amplified)

Adult Children.   There are times when we
have found ourselves living with children or siblings
whom we have raised to young adults who continue to
remain in our homes after becoming independent in
their own financial support. If we have not taught
them, they may fail to see why they should now start
contributing financially into the home's budget since
they've always received from us since birth or
fostering. This ball is now in our court. We must
show them we love them and want to prepare them for
the real world by easing them into the accountability
stage so when they move to their first apartment or
home they are not shocked by the many underlying
expenses that they had never before considered. This
assessment should be gradual (i.e. $200, monthly, first
year; $250, monthly, second year, etc.) and a docu-

mented, consistent amount not based on what they have left over after paying bills they've created but an amount that represents the second priority in a typical budget plan: Priority 1--Tithe, Priority 2--Housing.

Adult Siblings and Relatives. Some adult siblings will fall under the same category as your adult children if you have raised them. Refer to the above paragraph for guidance on them. Other adult siblings will fall under the same category as adult relatives because these two types usually come to stay with you as adults raised in other homes who are just staying for a period of time to relocate, geographically, or for some other short to long-term reasons. These individuals should also be assessed, accordingly.

We remember in Scripture how Israel let some of the inhabitants of the land continue to live there, against God's commandment to make no league with them, *"And ye shall make no league with the inhabitants of this land; and ye shall throw down their altars..." (Judges 2:2a).* The LORD knew that, in time, they would begin to take on their pagan ways, gradually turning their sons and daughters away from following God to serve other gods. However, they didn't obey God and He eventually saw their faithfulness to Him become lukewarm, then diluted, then polluted by mixture in their lifestyles (Deu 7:4; Josh 15:63, 16:10, 17:12; Judges 1:21, 27-35). Consequently, since Israel chose of their own free will to let the inhabitants (those whose hearts were not toward God) remain, the LORD did not forcibly drive them out, *"...but ye have not obeyed my voice: why have ye done this?...I will not drive them out from before you: but they shall be as thorns in your sides, and their gods shall be a snare unto you (Judges 2:2b-3).*

We see this same kind of lukewarmness practiced in many Christian homes today due to mixture tolerated in compromising lifestyles of adults in our homes who will not abide by our rules and laws which are based on the Word of God. Many times, such individuals change the values of our young children and cause them to even rebel against our rules. How do you get around this type of infiltration? Set an overall rule that's based on God's rule:

> **Our home is established on the biblical principle of two leaderships, the rule of the husband/father and the law of the wife/mother, one being dominant over the other (see Chapter 11). Any adults residing in our home (adult children, siblings, parents, relatives, etc.) will abide by these rules and laws. Noncompliance Scripturally gives us grounds for eviction from God's premises.**

You will find, at times, that God will send an individual to your home who is not walking in His will, yet, they are to live with you for a period of time for their spiritual growth. This may seem like a time of persecution for you till you begin to let God use you in molding them through much prayer, fasting, temperance, patience, godliness, brotherly kindness, and charity (II Peter 1:5-7). The LORD bountifully graced me to serve in this capacity for a period of time to individuals He was calling forth from varying captivities. If you have ever asked the LORD to teach you to be patient, kind, and charitable, and one such individual comes your way, it's just God answering your prayers.

Sick Persons. When your parents become elderly and can no longer care for themselves without assistance, by all means the LORD expects you to take them in, in their helpless state just as they nurtured you in your helpless state (as a baby). This paragraph is for all other type sicknesses of adult boarders listed in this section. If they are working or drawing any other kind of income (i.e. retirement, unemployment, medical disability, social security, pensions, etc.) they need to contribute to the household expenses. Their contribution should also be assessed according to previously mentioned rates. Some people are always sickly, it seems. You hate to even ask them, "How are you doing today?" This is because many sicknesses are spiritually based and won't be relieved until that spiritual deficiency is dealt with by them (slothfulness, rejection, fear of abandonment, etc.). Your repeatedly pitying them is just getting in the way of God bringing this self-pity, self-centeredness, or generational sin to the surface that they might deal with it once and for all. If they have no form of support and you think they may fall under the category in the above paragraph seek God for wisdom and also the church counsel established by your pastor.

"Where no counsel is, the people fall: but in the multitude of counsellors there is safety." Prov 11:14

"Without counsel purposes are disappointed: but in the multitude of counselors they are established." Prov 15:22

Some people don't want to work nor be well. While serving administratively in another church some years ago, I was handling a call to a public utility to verify an amount on an individual's account who was receiving assistance from us. The utility teller just said, *"Not again. Another church!"* This person was "church hopping" to pay monthly utilities. The individual you are helping could be "house hopping." Just be cognizant as you attempt to use wise counsel and discretion when opening up your home to others.

Those Who Don't Fit Any of the Above Categories. Adult siblings, two or more friends living together, and other biblically wholesome living arrangements can also glean some helpful guidance from this section on managing the traffic that flows in and out of your home and lives.

When Eviction Must be Considered. When you find that all effort to encourage your boarder's accountability to undergird his part of the household living expenses have availed no positive response or commitment from him, then you have no choice but to execute serious eviction proceedings. Please do this with the proper forewarnings to indicate to him your generosity in time given him to comply. A sample Eviction Notice that I served to a long-term visiting relative is provided in Appendix B. It was professionally served and enforced several years ago and even today we are on amiable terms with gained respect for me and the statutes of God.

CHAPTER 14

CONCLUSIVE BUDGET ACTIONS

A WORD OF WARNING!!!

God is calling us to stewardship and discipline before He imparts any divine disbursement. Will you heed the warning or will you be weeping and gnashing your teeth?

> *"....you should have invested my money with the bankers, and at my coming I could have received what was my own with interest. So take the talent away from him, and give it to the one who has ten talents. For to everyone who has will more be given, and he will be furnished richly so that he will have abundance, but from the one who does not have, even what he does have shall be taken away. And throw the good-for-nothing servant into the outer darkness; there will be weeping and grinding of teeth."* Matthew 25:27-30   (Amplified)

REPENTANCE FROM FINANCIAL SINS

The first step in making your budget work is **Repentance for Financial Sins** that:
- That which is God's shall not be taken from us and given to another. (Matthew 25:27-30)
- We might stop weeping and grinding our teeth.
- We might flee youthful lusts. (II Tim 2:22, Deu 14:25-26)
- We might not continue to oppose ourselves. (II Tim 2:25)
- We might recover ourselves out of the snare of the devil, who has taken us captive. (II Tim 2:26)

149

IT'S ALL ABOUT GOD

It is my desire that in meekness you receive the revelation the LORD brings forth in this book, that your financial management skills might become spiritually empowered. I Corinthians 3:6 says, *"I planted, Apollos watered, but God [all the while] was making it grow, and [He] gave the increase."* *(Amplified)* I have planted, now YOU GO and WATER it that God may give YOU the INCREASE.

Selah!

PART III:

PORTRAITS OF TRUE SPIRITUAL PROSPERITY

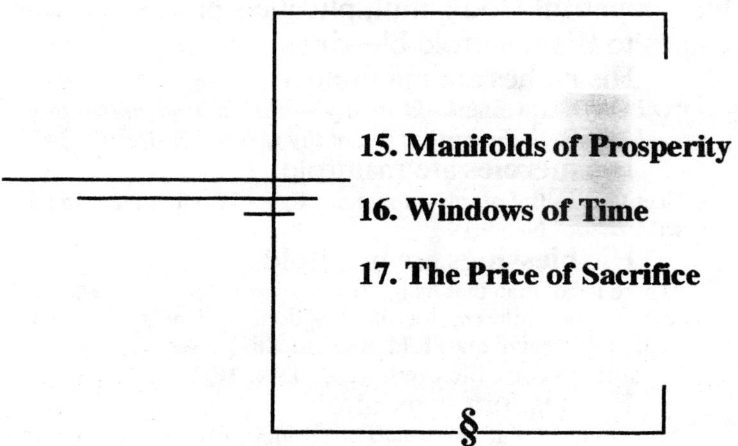

§

CHAPTER 15

MANIFOLDS OF PROSPERITY

MANIFOLDS ARE SCRIPTURAL

When the Bible speaks of "manifolds" it is making reference to diversity and infinite variety; it is reflective of the many-sided views and various forms of the subject being addressed. Manifolds consist of many of one kind, combined. This term goes even further to place emphasis on receiving many times more in this world; therefore, it speaks of the innumerable aspects which one form can take. With these descriptive phrases in mind, let's consider, Scripturally, just how bountiful God's multiplication process is, when it comes to His manifold blessings:

His **riches** are manifold.

*"O LORD, how **manifold** are thy works! In wisdom hast thou made them all: the earth is full of thy riches." Psalm 104:24*

His **mercies** are manifold.

"Yet thou in thy **manifold** mercies forsookest them not in the wilderness." Neh 9:19

His **blessings** are manifold.

"There is no man that hath left house, or parents, or brethren, or wife, or children, for the kingdom of God's sake, who shall not receive **manifold** more in this present time, and in the world to come life everlasting." Luke 18:29b-30

His **wisdom** is manifold.

"To the intent that now unto the principalities and powers in heavenly places, might be known by the church the **manifold** wisdom of God..." Ephesians 3:10

His **grace** is manifold.

"As every man hath received the gift, even so minister the same one to another, as good stewards of the **manifold** grace of God." I Peter 4:10

As we read these Scriptural representations of the LORD's manifolds we can readily see that He can make prosperity a many-sided wonder to our finite minds. As I experienced manifolds of prosperity, the LORD led me in and out of various "windows of time" which caused me to realize that many times we miss God because of poor timing, delayed obedience, and fear. As I began to mature in understanding God's "windows of time", I then too realized that these windows also applied to prosperity opportunities. The next few passages will share a few personal experiences with you as the Lord Jesus Christ led me through the windows of the office (seedtime), the farm (field time) then to ministry (harvest time). First, let's gain an understanding of the concept of windows.

UNDERSTANDING GOD'S
WINDOWS OF OPPORTUNITY

Have you every wondered why we call the computer software application which lets you access any program on your main menu screen "Windows"? It's because if you "go through" a particular window by clicking on it, you will open up a whole new group of screen choices with many more applications in them. BUT you must first go through a particular window on the main menu screen to gain access to the features housed within it. These "windows of opportunity" give you access while the main menu is up, before the screen-saver comes on due to idleness, before the computer automatically shuts down due to idleness, and before any other interference occurs. This is an interactive networking process that only benefits to its fullest (maximizes its opportunity to gain you access to all possible operations) when the right boxes are clicked, when certain documents are closed and opened, and when you read and follow the

153

instructions in the operator's manual.

Sometimes God would divinely arrange that you be the recipient of a prosperity opportunity that is just an initial window of opportunity for you to enter a higher spiritual plane of supernatural anointing, bountifulness, service to Him and trust in Him, without question. Yet, God makes such windows available when we are walking in His "perfect will" versus "permissive will".

A WINDOW OF OPPORTUNITY
FOR GOD'S PERFECT WILL
TO BE ACCOMPLISHED

About a month before God had spoken to me that He would uproot me from where I was and plant me in another state, a lady came to me and said the Lord showed her a vision of my home.

In the vision, she had entered the home and seen a large piano in my living room. She remembered seeing an integral garage and its door and also a building under construction in the backyard.

I wasn't particularly struck by the vision for I knew she had never been to my home and that she perhaps wanted to visit. I invited her over soon thereafter. As she walked into the living room she said, "Yes, that's the piano I saw." Then, she remembered the stairwell that took us downstairs and the garage. The only thing she didn't see was the unconstructed building.

After her short visit the Lord began to deal with me about moving to a neighboring state where I had been commuting to, bi-weekly, to minister to another lady confined for uncontrollable demonic activity (labeled schizophrenia). He spoke to my spirit that the lady's vision was a sign, for her family was to move into my house. Well, this was quite a twist in my future plans for I had planned to pay off this house within a few short years and complete the financing of my children's college education, now ongoing, but I did what I usually do when the Lord speaks: I moved with definite determination to obey.

A few weeks following the lady's visit I purposed to speak with their family because she was married to a minister who had been out West on church business during her first visit. When I visited them I learned that the LORD was truly orchestrating this situation because they were in the process of starting a church in the area and had actually recently begun having Services within their apartment. They had even been looking for a home to buy but their current consideration had fallen through, yet they were continuing to seek where God wanted them to move. They were looking for a particular type of house in which they could offer private rooming facilities to visiting ministers/prophets (like an Elisha room built onto the Shulamite's home). They had somewhat described my house for I had an apartment type area downstairs with its own bath and kitchen. Yet, I kept quiet.

I later visited one of their house Services and was surprised to learn that the only attendees other than themselves were myself and the two visitors I brought. When I returned home, the Lord showed me that the unconstructed building she saw in my backyard was their church building for out of the home ministry that He would ordain from within my home (in the garage which she vividly remembered) would be birthed a church that would rapidly multiply. By now a month had passed and they still had found no place to move; sensing it was my time to share with them what the LORD had shown me about their ministry, I invited the family over - dad, mom, and two young babes (9 mo. and 2 yr. old) - escorted them through my ten room, 2500 sq. ft. home and shared what the Lord had shown me.

I then didn't hear from them for a while for the minister had taken other travels. As another month rolled by, the LORD's timing pressed in my spirit. I was yielded to give them the piano (which was so new that I was still making payments on it at that time) and even sell the house at below market value to compensate their financial situation for he did not work; her income sustained their household. Weeks passed. When I still didn't hear from them, the LORD said to put the house on the market. (Remember, a motivational giver doesn't put pressure on people because the motivation is from God; see Chapter 8.) Right after the realtor placed the "For Sale" sign in the yard, the LORD spoke to my spirit, "I will take you out quickly". The next day the realtor brought a nurse and police officer by (spiritually representing deliverance and enforcement) who offered an immediate contract at my unnegotiable price.

That week, before accepting their offer, I visited the Church Services of the young ministering couple for I had learned that they had moved their Services from their apartment (in a neighboring city) to a nursery around the corner from my home for God had shown them they would be ministering in this area. I was a little late finding the place, yet they were happy to see me. I was yet even more concerned for their only attendee, other than their two little children, was me. When the Services were over, the young minister said that through his travels he had received a word from a prophet that the LORD would give them a new house, much larger than mine, and a Mercedes Benz. The next day I accepted the couple's offer whom the Lord had sent and was planted in the State God had directed me to go within a few short weeks.

A few months later, I received a telephone call from the minister's wife at my new residence. They were still residing in their apartment. (Please do come back and re-read this section after you have read, **Crossing Over the Bridge to True Spiritual Prosperity** in Chapter 17.)

CHAPTER 16

WINDOWS OF TIME

ENTERING & EXITING WINDOWS OF TIME

We all must travel through the many, many "Windows of Time" : the birth canal, the door that opens to our first grade class, the hallways that take us through the ranks of high school and college, the door we enter through to our honeymoon suite, the pathways through our children's lives, and the coffin door that shuts as we are last viewed by our loved ones as we depart this earth. I just hope you take the time, as you travel through these many "Windows of Time", to respond to every God-given opportunity to enter and exit every higher plane of spiritual advancement that the Lord has set in your path to lead you into the supernatural anointing and bountifulness that He has purposed for you as you serve Him and trust in Him, without question.

GOD PRESENTS OPPORTUNITIES

The LORD presents many opportunities in our lives. It is up to us to pursue and seize them and then walk in them. God presented opportunities in my life to become a giver, to become a receiver and to get out of the box.

OPPORTUNITIES TO DEVELOP AS A GIVER

The most challenging incident in my development as a giver was not the most sacrificial one but the one which required absolute faith because a pressing bill was due at the time God gave the faith call. I had approximately $6,500 in college expenses due for one semester for one of my children. I usually paid the semester bills with a combination of cash, scholarship, and financial aid, when necessary. This semester we sought no assistance because we had submitted a change in state residency package that would have shifted us into the category of being able to pay the entire bill in full, per semester; however, our state residency consideration was denied for the coming semester. Meanwhile, I had paid $2,500 on the up-coming semester bill with the remaining amount being pastdue. I did not have the $4,000 to clear up this past due amount. Within a few weeks of paying the $2,500, the LORD told me to invest $500 in a particular ministry. I did not have the money but the following week I had planned to pay $500 on the school bill when I got paid from my job; however, instead of paying this amount on the bill I sowed it into that ministry. Two months later (and 30 days before we would be dismissed from the school for non-payment of the bill), the residency denial was reversed and that $4,000 note turned into a $600+ credit!

OPPORTUNITIES TO DEVELOP
AS A RECEIVER

I was involved in a car accident which ended up with my car being totaled after being hit by a tractor-trailer, with a second impact coming from slamming into the wall at 55 mph and launched back into on-coming traffic, head-on. This accident had more than natural implications; yet, I'll just address the "receiv-ing" report here. The LORD allowed me to miracu-lously walk away without even being shakened. The trucking company supplied me a rental car for three weeks but wanted to settle with me on the car for face value since it was old, registering over 120,000 miles. (This is the car in chapter 12, under Car Repair/Maintenance, that registered 84,000 miles when I purchased it.)

I refused the report of death. The problem was, with two children in college, I didn't need a car payment and this car was a gift from God just two years prior. God plunged me into deeper faith of receiving the ridiculous when He awakened me the Saturday morning before I had to give up the rental car. He told me to go out to the car yard they had towed it to and anoint it. Well, it was broad daylight and I didn't know who would be there and how to get through if no one was there, etc., etc., etc. but I got up and went. When I arrived, I found the car sitting outside the locked gate. (They thought it was such a heap of metal that it wasn't even valuable enough to secure.) I took my oil and raised that car from the dead just like my Heavenly Father said! The following week, the man who owned the car yard called me to say he thought he could fix that car with some old parts. When I contacted the trucker's insurance company they released the settlement check and the car, still settling for face value of the car. By the end of that week I had a like new car for the repairman said he couldn't find old parts so he had to get new parts from the dealership yet he still accepted the small check from the insurance company in full payment.

My yielding to receive an aged Chevrolet Celebrity allowed God to restore it to travel over 258,000 miles, almost 140, 000 more miles after it rose from the dead! Just 6 months ago, the LORD led me to bless another family with it who didn't have a car. They are still driving it today, purring beautifully with a heavenly hummmmmmmm. God is ready for us to learn to receive in things that seem impossible for it takes great faith to contently receive what seems old and dead as a blessing rather than the curse it was intended to be.

COMING OUT OF THE BOX

The world system has coined the phrase "coming out of the box" to refer to coming out of timidity, bringing out your personality, etc. We're going to look at it from a supernatural aspect for when God brought me out of the box in 1996 it was truly a supernatural experience. When we do a Scripture search, we find that in every instance, there was a precious substance locked away in the box, **Anointing Oil**. Let's look at all these references:

• Elisha the prophet had Jehu anointed with a box of oil when Jehu was anointed to do the work that the LORD had called him to. *"...take the box of oil and pour it on his head..." II Kings 9:1-3*

• Mary Magdalene anointed the Lord Jesus with precious ointment from an alabaster box. *"...an alabaster box of ointment of spikenard very precious...brake the box and poured it on his head..." Matt 26:7, Mark 14:3*

• Mary Magdalene in another occasion anointed the Lord Jesus ' feet with precious ointment from an alabaster box. *"...brought an alabaster box of ointment...his feet and anointed them with the ointment. Luke 7:37-38*

In each of these instances there is something spiritual happening.

-- Jehu was released to go smite the house of King Ahab and avenge the blood of the LORD's servants, shed at the hand of Jezebel.

-- The Lord Jesus' body was anointed for burial in release to shed His blood for the covering of our sins in the Matthew and Mark references.

-- Mary Magdalene was released from her many sins in the Luke reference.

In each case, there was something precious **bound up** in a box that had the capability of releasing something else even more powerful once released from the box. A box is a container made to do just that, **contain** its contents. The noun form of the word box describes it as a **small compartment.** The verb form means to **enclose in**. Why even the area of the body that was anointed placed spiritual emphasis on the ministry work which followed:

-- **The Hands = your empowerment to Do.**

The hands that were used to do the anointing represent ones power to labor and get wealth.

-- **The Head = your empowerment to Be.**

The head represents the real "you" -- the mind, the place where spiritual wisdom, which is seated* in your spirit, and natural wisdom, which is seated* in your intellect, meet and synthesize; thus, the anointing of the Head represents the setting apart of the real "you". Therefore, it is very important to always keep it covered, spiritually. (Eccles 9:8b)

-- **The Feet = your empowerment to Go.**

The feet represent your ministry; thus, the anointing of your feet represents your ability to accomplish that ministry work.

Ancient kings recognized this parallel; that's why, when they captured and bound military leaders from the enemy's camp, they bound their hands with chains and their feet with fetters of iron and brass:

- II Sam 3:34
- Ps 105:18, 149:8
- Mark 5:4
- Luke 8:29

*(Two seats, referring to a spiritual man whose spirit and soul have been severed, Heb 4:12.)

THE PARALLEL BETWEEN BEING RELEASED FROM YOUR JOB & INDEBTEDNESS AND GOING FORTH TO DO MINISTRY

You may be wondering by now, "What does all this mean for me? Simply this: today, Satan would have you ignorant to the fact that if you are bound up by your job and financial indebtedness, you are not released to move forward into effective ministry for the Lord Jesus Christ! Now get this point well, for this may be your moment of release: Satan knows if you allow him to bind your hands, mind and feet, you can not go forward! Meditate on this point, consider and be WISE!

If God has a spiritual calling in your life, the financial securities of your job just may be a hindrance. Of course, if you have a family and children, God will allow a smooth transition from the world system to complete dependence on Him. He did it for me and at a time when He knew I had two children in college. The basic spiritual points you need to remember when accepting a change in your life concerning your release from trust in worldly resources and coming into a total dependency on God are these:

1. <u>You can not go forth until the anointing comes</u>. (box=your job, oil=your Holy Spirit anointing)

2. <u>Oil can not be effective just sitting in the box</u>. (trusting in the job more than God will leave the anointing to do ministry in a box with an unbroken seal.)

3. <u>Oil must be applied to activate</u>. (If the ministry God called you to do lies dormant because of overtime, two jobs, too many bills, the oil can not be applied, nor ministry activated.)

4. <u>Oil, when activated, will bring forth a release.</u>

(Once all spider webs from the world system have been cut, you are ready for the anointing and release to do ministry.)

THE CONCEPT OF
SOMETHING PRECIOUS IN A BOX

This concept of something precious being released from a box is very important here because we must first see that a box confines its contents before we can realize that there's a supernatural struggle between our worldly jobs (the box) holding us in and our spiritual calling (the anointing oil) releasing us, bringing us forth out of the box.

The end result of whether we will stay in the box or not will depend upon two things:

(1) Our ability over our flesh's desire to stay in the box. Our flesh depends on the security of the money we receive from these jobs. Yet, this security hinders us from stepping out to be freed up to follow God's ministry calling. It fears losing the security of benefits in exchange for walking in faith that God will continue to keep us as we walk the narrow bridge of testing and proving to advance from the security of the four corners (every office building has four basic corners.) into the open space of abounding in all things and doing all things through Christ who strengthens us.

(2) How we respond to people who try to keep us in the box or put us back in when God has taken us out. These are those who are your friends. They don't want you to leave the box because they are afraid to leave the box. They say "Amen" to everything you say about God's calling but are afraid to get their feet wet from wading in the heckling from the crowd when they hear what material possessions you gave up to follow the LORD's calling. So, when they see you go up (out of the box) they pull you back down (in the box); then, sometimes jealousy is the root of people holding on to you. Then once out of the box you must only go in the direction that God has planned for you. You've got to be careful. When God has call-ed you out of a secular job or from one ministry area to another that He specifies to you as a higher calling, you've got to be focused. You must :

•Obey God no matter what. He will be respon-sible for the consequences of your obedience.

•Learn to trust God for everything you need.

•Learn to wait on the Lord for His direction and timing. God is in absolute control of every circum-stance of life. You've got to depend upon the Holy Spirit for everything; therefore, it is imperative that you make your personal prayer and meditation time the first priority of each day.

•GO DO THE MINISTRY HE HAS CALLED YOU TO DO.

I said all the above to make this short statement: When God finally called me off my job, He said to me, "I'm taking you out of the box, GO". I had to make the steps and choose between flesh and spirit, comfort and change, ministry and ministry. It was difficult because I had to pull off some sticky spider webs that were clinging to me, some in the form of money, people, job assignments that, "*...no one else can do but you, we need you*", even, some in the form of successful ministry that went along with the old place that made me feel successful in accomplishing the LORD's work. But I made my step, I'm out of the box and I've avoided all sticky webs to pull me into a new box.

CHAPTER 17

THE PRICE OF SACRIFICE

TRANSFERENCE IN FINANCIAL COVERING

"For where your treasure is, there will your heart be also."
Matthew 6:21

From reading Chapter 6, **Financial Coverings**, we see that the Word of God has already established our coverings: God over Christ, the Son; Christ over the man; and the man over the woman. When we are single parents, we have wedged a brokenness, a breach in our relationship with God that must still conform, in a direct way, with the pattern God has established in His divine order of spiritual coverings.

When I was a single parent of two children for 18 years ('78-'96) I found my financial coverings in my ex-husband through child support, salary from my job and part-time administrative work at my church (then $60,000+), my $325,000+ life insurance coverage, health and other insurance, retirement fund, individual retirement account, home and personal properties, and other material possessions. When I gave my life to Christ Jesus in September 1982, I accepted Him as my all-encompassing covering over these smaller umbrellas of security and, as I am a human being living in a complex society, He left these smaller coverings intact. Then in 1996, the LORD required all of these financial coverings of me, dissolving them, connecting my ex-husband's covering directly with our daughter who was still in college and investing all else in ministry work, as the LORD saw fit. He then placed me back under my dad's covering for a period of time ('96 -'98), then under my church's covering

('97-'98), then directly under His supernatural financial covering ('98)*. It was then when the LORD transferred me from natural to supernatural covering (for all the previous coverings were natural, even that of the church) that it required much faith. Little did I know that this was the bridge over which I had to cross to reach the prosperity anointing.

PROSPERITY ANOINTING

The prosperity anointing unleashes you from binding captivity in areas that have been hindered, now freed up to prosper. When the wicked are in power there is hindrance, when they are removed there is a release (Prov 29:2). Thus, when satanic oppressions exist over your finances, your resources are stifled. When his stronghold is broken your resources are released to flow without hindrance. The Word of God prospered (grew, multiplied and prevailed) after King Herod died (Acts 12:20-24) and after witchcraft books were burned during Paul's ministry in Ephesus (Acts 19:19-20). The prosperity anointing isn't all about money. It's spiritual. It's about God's manifold blessings in every area of your life. Just look at some of the areas through which the prosperity anointing causes yield:

•**real estate property**
"...all the land which thou seest, to thee will I give it."
(Gen 13:15)

•**blessings upon children and descendants**
"...I will make thy seed as the dust of the earth..."
(Gen 13:16)

•**material possessions**
"...the LORD hath blessed my master greatly...flocks... herds...silver...gold..." (Gen 24:35)

---

*This is not to say that I'm not under any man's covering for I am currently under my pastor's covering. The transfer here is in reference to the manner in which I was financially supported at the time.

• favor (from Boaz to Ruth)
"...The Lord recompense thy work and a full reward be given thee..." (Ruth 2:12-13)
• benefits
"Bless the LORD...forget not all His benefits."
(Ps 103:2)
• childbearing fruitfulness
"...the fruit of the womb is His reward...Thy wife...a fruitful vine...thy children like olive plants..."
(Ps 127:3-5, 128:3-6)
• whatever you set forth your hands to do
"...the LORD made all that he (Joseph) did to prosper in his hand." (Gen 39:3)
• a good name that will proceed you
(Solomon, I Kings 10:7)
• wisdom in dealing with people
(Solomon, I Kings 10:8)
• hindrance removed; increase brought forth
"...ground shall give her increase...I will cause the remnant...to possess." (Zech 8:12)
• 30 fold, 60 fold, 100 fold blessing
(Gen 26:12; Matt 13:8, 19:29, Mark 4:8, 10:29-30)

SHOWERS OF THE
PROSPERITY ANOINTING

The bestowing of the prosperity anointing is gradual. The LORD sprinkled showers upon me while my home was still intact. You can read the details of many of these in the book, *Raising Responsible Children In A Single Parent Home*. Yet, I'd like to share the inception of what I will call the "initial shower" here.

When I had lost the opportunity to acquire a promotion on a particular job because of a whistle blower mission God had sent me on, the LORD spun my family into prosperous situations that defied Satan's effort, through man, to place a stronghold on my God ordained pre-destination to prosper. After a God-ordained 35 day Fast during that challenging mission, the Lord showed me a short vision of my right hand around the throat of a python snake. The LORD later sent me to a management college in which I stayed in a luxurious executive hotel plaza, joined by my then teen-aged daughter during the summer months; during the same time He sent my son overseas to several European countries as a US Student Ambassador.

The following year, the LORD sent my daughter to Germany for a month experiencing exchange student and Christian family life in fellowship with a Holy Spirit filled church there. That same year the LORD sent me to Colorado where He had a powerful Word for me at a Christian Music Seminar during which God used a professional music artist, laying on hands, to speak Isaiah 61:1 over me,

"The spirit of the LORD GOD is upon me; because the Lord hath anointed me to...bind up the brokenhearted, to proclaim liberty to the captives, and the opening of the prison to.... (the) .... bound."

Paralleling the bringing forth of this prophecy the Lord began to develop the spiritual gifts of discerning of spirits, word of wisdom, and word of knowledge which changed my music ministry tremendously. My daughter was later designated a Congressional Scholar, spending a week with congressmen, political figures and other national scholars in the nation's Capital. Later that year, she was designated a model United Nations representative, representing Australia and Canada. Both children went on to complete undergraduate degrees at nationally well-known colleges, the University of Virginia and the University of North Carolina at Chapel Hill with funds which God supernaturally manifested as He truly called forth *"...the treasures of darkness, and hid-*

den riches of secret places..." (Isaiah 45:3); for just the year prior to their college years, I remember my son asking one school morning, *"Mom, how are we going to go to college when you can't even give us lunch money?"* ; Yet, within just five short years after he had made this statement, I had paid over $50,000 of college notes, in cash, and upon liquidating my possessions to follow God's call to move, I'd amassed over $100,000 more to invest in the Kingdom of God.

THE SPLENDOR OF
THE WILDERNESS

After transferring all my goods to the LORD and moving to where He had reassigned me, I seemed to go through a wilderness period as I worked as a laborer on a vegetable farm ('96-'97), yet even the crops began to prosper for where I laid my hands, the vines kept yielding fruit. In fact, some spring crops were still yielding produce in the fall when the fall crop was ready and I had to work both fields simultaneously. I remember one farmer giving up his patch of cucumbers to the one I was laboring for because it would not bring forth a yield. My farmer asked me to glean what I could from that patch while he ran to the market. When he had returned a couple of hours later, I had picked over five bushels and had not finished the patch ! When the neighboring farmer discovered the yield he retrieved the patch!

The LORD required much lengthy fasting during these days for much spiritual opposition to my presence in that geographical area was present as I entered areas and Christian fellowships oppressed by witchcraft control. My presence was not welcomed by the demonic evil spirits nor their human counterparts, yet I was there to labor for the LORD. The LORD Jesus taught me a tremendous amount about spirituality among the many plants, insects, animals and territorial happenings on the open land around me. As I learned lessons from even what the earth, river, trees, etc. would speak to my spirit man, I saw why God would place me in the fields as a laborer of natural things (while doing some ministry work in church, of course) before going directly to full time spiritual labor in that area.

*".....The first man Adam was made a living soul; the last Adam was made a quickening spirit. Howbeit that was not first which is spiritual, but that which is **natural; and afterward that which is spiritual**...as we have borne the image of the earthy, we shall also bear the image of the heavenly." I Cor 15:45-49)*

At first it was fun to see the blessings of the LORD on the crops which kept yielding beyond their expectancy, yet as the year wore on I became delighted to see the "killer frost" which was suppose to kill all vegetation, yet some still seemed to brave that strongman and come back in mid-winter!

While laboring in the fields, I was active at church and in the community where God sent people my way to lay hands on certain financial needs. I didn't realize this was God, until I saw a pattern of individuals coming out of financial bondage -- many of those, spiritual captivity -- which required acknowledgment, repenting of sins, breaking of curses, and the application of time-sensitive, God focused financial wisdom which caused a major turn around in their budget plans. This was God-directed ministry work which required much intercession which in turn revealed many spiritual sources of financial problems.

The entire time God used me in these areas to help others I was living with the basics in life as a laborer on a farm. The splendor of it all is, today the LORD Jesus Christ is breaking fetters of iron and chains of bondage off those who have the faith to believe in and apply what the LORD's Word purports about the spiritual and natural matters concerning our stewardship over His finances. God has richly imparted spiritual blessings of prosperity immeasurably beyond the financial; yet, many get so caught up in the love of the <u>prosperity</u> rather than the love of the <u>Prosperer</u>, the Lord Jesus Christ, that we must now look at the grave area of false prophecy that fuels the prosperity movement thriving in the churches, today.

CROSSING OVER THE BRIDGE TO
TRUE SPIRITUAL PROSPERITY

We must remember that money is what makes the world system function and because of that, Satan has used much yielding to false prophecy to steal away hearts of those who are not truly committed to the cross to whore after the riches rather than the desire to release it to ministry work. This is why God cannot give the prosperity anointing to every Christian. Satan will place a deceived Christian with a false prophet, one who prophesies through information received from demon spirits rather than from the Holy Spirit. Since the world system is propelled by money and materialism (mammon) he can actually make this false prophecy appear to come true when, in essence, demons are used to deliver these alluring goods which this deceived Christian so lusted after, whose lust is revealed from the change in his Christian walk after the fulfilling of that false prophecy:

*"If there arise among you a prophet, or a dreamer of dreams, and giveth thee a sign or a wonder, and **the sign or the wonder come to pass**, whereof he spake unto thee, saying, Let us go after other gods, which thou hast not known, and let us serve them; thou shalt not hearken unto the words of that prophet, or that dreamer of dreams: for the LORD your God proveth you, to know whether ye love the LORD your God with all your heart and with all your soul."*   Deu 13:1-3

I preface this paragraph with this strong point because I don't have a desire for money and its riches. I asked the LORD for the kind of gifted spiritual anointing the prophets and the apostles had in the Bible -- that of Moses, Elijah, Elisha, Daniel, Peter, John, Paul, and many others who walked so closely with the LORD that they could touch Him, see His hinder parts, lay in His bosom. God said, *"That'll cost you a lot."*

Then the LORD put me in the position to watch an aged prophet (perhaps deceived, perhaps disobedient)* minister to a group of people prophesying material prosperity with no significant emphasis on repentance or salvation over a period of two weeks of nightly Services. The Lord placed me in this position by telling me to attend a certain type of Christian gathering which I usually would not have attended (I only support the existing pastor the LORD places me under with my physical attendance.); yet, this one time the LORD said He had something He wanted me to observe there. So, I attended most Services nightly, covered by the blood of Jesus. The Lord Jesus Christ told me to give him a sacrificial offering, not disclosing that it was such for only God knew that it was indeed sacrificial (It was all that I had.).

As I slept the night before I purposed to give this sacrificial offering, the Lord Jesus showed me a vision of my approaching the altar of this particular Service in a line of people. In the vision, as I handed the prophet my offering, he said, *"And what do you desire, my child?"* to which I replied, *"I want twice the*

Many false prophets are devoted worshippers of Satan from the inception of their false ministry work. Others become false prophets through falling away from what was once true ministry work. Such false prophets, through lusting after blessings received from God during years of service as a true prophet, will FIRST fall away as a disobedient prophet before complete apostasy. I Kings 13, II Kings 23:16-18 *anointing that you have and I'll use it right for God's work."* Then, I awakened. The next day, I gave my sacrificial offering. Not knowing what the Lord had personally spoken to me in the vision and in the days before, this prophet stopped me when I approached the altar to give my sealed-envelope offering, and prophesied, *"The LORD says, you want something different*. The Lords says, He's going to give it to you and He's still going to prosper you."*

When I returned to my seat (in the last row) and the prophet returned to his prophecies of material prosperity the LORD prompted me to leave for I had received what He had purposed for me to receive. As I walked through the rear exit, I heard the prophet noticeably stumble in his prophecy as he was speaking prosperity over the person standing before him. As I turned, the LORD spoke to my spirit man, *"The anointing has passed."*

Nine months later, after relinquishing my home, job, and other sacrificial renderings to the LORD, I laid on the floor of my empty 10 room house, scheduled to move out early the next day with just a baby grand piano sitting in the living room, beautifully reflecting on the recently polished hardwood floor. As I peacefully drifted off to sleep in the still quietness, I pondered God's commission to me to sacrificially decrease amid a stream of prophecies of increase spoken over others. Then, around 3 a.m. that same early morning, the LORD awakened me. There was a tremendous anointing in the room as I just seemed to lay on the floor in a heat wave. Tears streamed from my eyes as I worshipped the LORD in due obeisance and reverence. Then, the LORD spoke to me to pick up my Bible and read (It always lays beside my head). I

**NOTE: All other prophecies coming forth to others there centered around things money could buy.*

picked up where I had left off, not connecting any events which had just occurred to those which had occurred nine months prior; the point at which the Holy Spirit quickened me,

"Behold, I have done according to thy words: lo, I have given thee a wise and an understanding heart; so that there was none like thee before thee, neither after thee shall any arise like unto thee. And I have also given thee that which thou hast not asked, both riches, and honour: so that there shall not be any among the kings like unto thee all thy days." I Kings 3:12-13

I continued in reverent obeisance to the Lord Jesus Christ yet remembering that the Bible said we are not to add to the Word of God (Deu 4:2, Prov 30:5-6, Rev 22:18-19). He then made me to understand Solomon's gifts of wisdom -- that spiritual and human wisdom needed to lead in dealing with earthly matters; thus, my wisdom gift would deal with spiritual and human wisdom needed in confronting with the dark powers of Satan in releasing captives and the spiritually oppressed. The LORD had added extraordinary wisdom and also riches, that which I had not asked. The Word speaks of 30 fold, 60 fold and 100 fold blessings. When I had completed transferring all my goods to Him in the manner He had directed, the LORD Jesus Christ spoke which blessing I would receive:

*"...There is no man that hath left house...children, or lands, for my sake, and the gospel's but he shall receive and **hundred-fold** now in this time...with **persecutions;** and in the world to come eternal life." Mark 10:29-30*

.....and He spoke of one more restoration that I will be silent about for now.

The spiritual essence of the prosperity anointing is that it's not for all Christians, that is, the prosperity anointing, not the ability to prosper, for one is broader than the other. I don't have the prosperity anointing because I wanted it. I don't desire riches. My heart's desire is toward kingdom work; kingdom ministry; God's will to be done in earth as it is in heaven; the operation of the ministry, motivational, and manifestation gifts; the release of the saints from the captivities of Satan through knowledge about areas in our lifestyles that are giving over ground to demonic spirits; and that when others look upon me that they are blinded to any human qualities God has given me that only the Glory of Christ Jesus is seen in full radiance on my face. So, if you truly covet the prosperity anointing make sure, before you ask God for it, that you are ready to say when He asks you, through His true prophet, *"Now what do you desire?"*, that you can honestly respond, *"I desire to help others, and die to self"*. If you can not respond with that ministry-focused response you are not ready to receive the prosperity anointing.

Lida Leech's tune *"Trust, Try and Prove Me"* is a melody that rings out so clearly the consecrated service God calls us to in giving of all to Him:

TRUST, TRY, and PROVE ME

verse 1

Bring ye all the tithes into the storehouse,
All your money, talents, time, and love;
Consecrate them all upon the altar,
While your Saviour from above speaks sweetly,
Trust Me, try Me, prove Me,
Saith the Lord of hosts,
And see if a blessing, unmeasured blessing,
I will not pour out on thee.

Lida S. Leech, 1873- ©1923, renewal 1951, Broadman Press

ONE HUNDRED FOLD BLESSINGS WITH PERSECUTION

"For it was not an enemy that reproached me.....but it was thou, a man mine equal, ...mine acquaintance......(who)....walked unto the house of God in company."
Psalm 55:12-14

I used to think this Scripture was addressing the increase in the entourage of satanic attacks you will face; the world system turning against you; oppression, suppression, and depression from the enemies of the Cross. Yet, I was dumbfounded to discover that most of my share of heart-piercing persecution would come from those Christian acquaintances who responded adversely to God's hand upon my life. *"Lord, do not hold this against them."*

TRUST, TRY, and PROVE ME
verse 3
I have yielded Him my life forever,
All I am, or have, or hope to be;
Naught on earth my hold on Him can sever,
While I hear Him say to me, My child,
Just trust Me, try Me, prove Me,
Saith the Lord of hosts,
And see if a blessing, unmeasured blessing,
I will not pour out on thee.
Lida S. Leech, 1873- ©1923, renewal 1951, Broadman Press

AFTERGLOW

*"Behold, I have taught you statutes and judgments, even as the LORD my God commanded me, that ye should do so in the land whither ye go to possess it. Keep therefore and do them: for this is your **wisdom** and your **understanding** in the sight of the nations, which shall hear all these statutes, and say, **Surely this great nation is a wise and understanding people.**" Deu 4:5-6*

It is an humbling delight to a true servant of God to see the fruit of the ministry which God has placed him in, blossom in the lives of those who faithfully walk in the Lord's obedience. Once you've offered up your financial stewardship to God, please do write me and let me know of the divine interventions you've experienced from operating under the umbrella of God's Word in the administration of your budget. With the confessing and forsaking of financial sins, you will experience supernatural help from Almighty God that will give you anointed wisdom to whittle down tremendous consumer debt, resolve past financial problems and settle financial breaches not resolved from the past.

May God grant you spiritual wisdom in dealing with the root problem of your financial concerns. May you gain financial wisdom in all areas of revelation that only God can impart to the spirit of him who wants to know and operate in the light of the truth of His Word. My desire for you is that God will divinely intervene and supernaturally render healing to financial situations in your life from just taking your stewardship seriously as a representative of God rather than just an owner of material possessions. I pray that you experience divine anointing, supernatural intervention, unmerited favor, spiritual multiplication, supernatural cancellation, and other graces from God due to your faithful application of the sound Biblical principles revealed in this book.

God does render manifold blessings, today, when we apply His universal and timeless resource management principles to financial situations facing modern-day Christian families.

As God has placed me in your path to *Plant*, now you GO and *Water*, and watch <u>GOD</u> give YOU the *INCREASE!*   I Corinthians 3:6

Dear Heavenly Father,

I pray that you richly bless those faithful Christian Families who read and apply the revelation knowledge You have commissioned me to share in this book. Cause them to see that Your promises are true when we order our finances according to the Scriptural disciplines you have established in Your Holy Word.

In Christian Service to "Christ"-ians,
Your servant,
Viola

APPENDIX A
BUDGET PLANNING FORMS

When you are ready to plan your own budget using the guidelines discussed in Chapter 12, I encourage you to purchase the planning guide, *Family Planner*, the companion workbook to this text. It is designed for serious record keeping when planning your own budget. The *Family Planner* includes such budgeting helps as --

    A Pocket-Sized Quad-Folded Grocery Checklist
    Budget Planning Worksheets
    Bi-Weekly Budget Plan Sheets
    Weekly Budget Plan Sheets
    Monthly Budget Plan Sheets
    Business Ledger Record and Expense Sheets

Once you've determined what monthly household expenses you actually have, you must lay them all out on paper to actually manage them. With these budget plan sheets, you will be able to map your way out of "Egypt" into a more prosperous lifestyle.

The Business Ledger Record and Expense Sheets are excellent tools for those who need a record keeping system when starting a small business at home. If you use this system, your busines will always show a profit and provide "seed" money for tithes and a sustaining a base for your business account.

So pick up the *Family Planner* to get a headstart on implementing the budgeting guidelines discussed in this text.

APPENDIX B
HOUSEHOLD RULES AND SCHEDULES

You'll find blank copies of household rules and schedules charts in the planning guide, *Family Planner*, the companion workbook to this text. Use them to begin to set your entire household on a disciplined, orderly and, most of all, Godly routine. The *Family Planner* will provide you with:

Weekly Self-Evaluation Charts -- for your child to assess himself & discuss with you.

Household Rules -- for assignment of chores and television watching schedules and for water conservation.

Energy Saving Tips -- on electricity and energy saving devices.

Your budget will not work if you are the only person in the house who's going to cut back and conserve resources. It takes the entire household.

A Sample Eviction Notice is provided on the next page for siblings, relatives and friends who reside in your home for an extended period of time, not paying, not following rules, negatively influencing your children, etc. (Of course, this doesn't include any sick or aged parents whom you are caring for.)

SAMPLE
EVICTION NOTICE

For:________________________________   25 Sep 98
223-00-9999   Auburn Hair
5' 7"   Light Brown Eyes

//

________________________________ is hereby evicted from the
residence of 12500 Richon Street, Terryville, Va 23451.

Eviction is pronounced due to the following reasons:
1. She did not complete all requirements for staying here,
although these were made known to her on the first day of
her entrance into our home. These requirements were also
reiterated in writing but yet ignored.

2. She has not made a conscientious, proactive, genuine
attempt to leave although her original statement, when
arriving for temporary shelter, was that she would only be
staying 2-3 days, rather than 2-3 years. Nor did she follow-
up on opportunities to pursue:
       - Classified Ads made available to her (19 Sep 98).
       - Name/Address/Phone # of her local blood relative.
       - Another Ad, 24 Sep 98.

//

____ originally left this
residence on 1 Aug 98, without prior notice to me, with damages to my
personal property.

____ is welcomed to make
future visits and telephone calls to me, as in the past.
    Further contacts ________________________________ may be
interested in:

Viola L. Britt
VIOLA L. BRITT
RESIDENCE STEWARD

APPENDIX C
SAMPLE LETTER RESOLVING JUDGEMENTS

A sample letter of acknowledgement of debt owed and an offer of genu-ine repentive measures to restore within your current financial means.

Allison Kallison
11111 Judge Street
Courtland, California 22222-0000
(111) 444-6666
1 January 1998

Myer's Used Car Dealership
Attention: Manager
Box 345
Businessville, Illinois 33333-0000

Dear Sir:

    I am writing concerning a debt I owe your dealership that was incurred back in 1990. I had purchased an '87 Mercury from you and never paid any of my payments. I was not prompt in making my first payment, planning to make a double payment the next month; however, the next month the car was totaled in an accident. Although judgement was served against me to pay the full amount due, I could not due to unemployment for an extended period of time. As years progressed and I gained employment, I never attempted to settle this bill.

    I was not a Christian then and didn't understand the need to honor my past debt as I do now. I ask your forgiveness for ignoring this debt for such a long time. I also ask that a payment schedule be set up that is within my financial means, preferably $30 a month or other arrangement we can mutually agree upon, due to current expenses and family obligations.

    You may reach me at the above address and phone number. Thank you for your time and assistance.

Sincerely,
Allison Kallison
Allison Kallison

C-1

APPENDIX D
STEWARDHIP APPLIED -
SCRIPTURAL PRINCIPLES ON THE
USE OF MONEY

---

1. <u>Anointing</u>. Your finances will be spiritually blessed when you become obedient to God's monetary laws.

Gen 26:12-16	Proverbs 8:21
I Kings 17:8-16	Isaiah 45:3
II Kings 4:1,7	Isaiah 55:1-2
I Chronicles 29:11-14	Malachi 3:10-12
Proverbs 3:9-10	Matthew 19:29
	Mark 10:29-30

2. <u>Borrowing</u> will bring you into bondage with the lender until you've settled that debt.

Exodus 22:14-15	Proverbs 22:7
Nehemiah 5:1-5	Isaiah 24:1-3
Psalms 37:21a	Romans 13:8

3. <u>Bankruptcy.</u> God does not endorse bankruptcy in the financial principles He sets forth in the Bible.

Psalms 15:4	Acts 5:4
Psalms 66:13,14	

4. <u>Contentment</u> with what you have left over after you've paid your bills is next to godliness.

Proverbs 15:16
Isaiah 58:11

5. <u>Curses</u> come upon your finances when not fulfilling some of your financial commitments. These curses include such things as financial loss, health problems,

emotional instability, and division in the home (especially when the "head" of the home "embezzles" God's money).

Leviticus 27:30-31	Proverbs 28:27
Deuteronomy 23:21-23	Ecclesiastes 5:4-6
Proverbs 28:13	Malachi 3:8-10
Jeremiah 17:5	

6. <u>Dishonesty</u> (Hypocrisy; Swindling) Treat people fairly in your financial dealings -- this includes minorities, women, children, your relatives and foreigners. A "swindler" is an abomination to God.

Leviticus 19:15	Proverbs 16:11
Deuteronomy 25:13-16	Proverbs 20:10, 23
Proverbs 11:1	Proverbs 20:14

7. <u>Employment</u>. You are supposed to expect financial gain from labor with your hands and mental faculties.

Genesis 3:19a
Proverbs 13:11b

8. <u>Fast-Cash</u>. Avoid get-rich-quick schemes.

Proverbs 23:4-5
Proverbs 28:20, 22

9. <u>Giving</u>. The first step in receiving is to give.

Leviticus 25:35	Proverbs 28:27
Deuteronomy 15:7-11	Proverbs 29:7
Psalms 37:21b	Ezekiel 18:5,7
Proverbs 3:27-28	Matthew 5:42
Proverbs 11:24a	Luke 6:38
Proverbs 13:7b	Luke 12:33-34
Proverbs 19:17	II Corinthians 8:9
Proverbs 21:26b	Philemon 18-19

10. <u>Gambling</u> -- Observing of times and chances. God

does not want to find among us any who observes times and chances. The lottery, stock market, jackpots, raffles, and some card and bingo games require you to speculate at a cost, putting some of God's money in first for a chance at winning.

Leviticus 19:26	Proverbs 13:11
Deuteronomy 18: 10, 14	Proverbs 23:4-5
II Kings 21:2, 6	Proverbs 28: 20, 22
II Chronicles 33:2, 6	Galatians 4:9-10

11.   <u>Hoarding</u>; Trusting Money. The Bible teaches against hoarding and seeking after money to resolve your financial problems. It causes you to become self-centered, covetous, and lustful for material gain. (The root of continuous financial problems is usually spiritual in nature.)

Psalms 115:4-8	Psalms 135:15-18
Proverbs 10:4	Zephaniah 1:18
Proverbs 11:24b	Matthew 6:19-21
Proverbs 11:28	Matthew 19:21-33
Proverbs 13:7a	Luke 12:15
Proverbs 23:4-5	Luke 12:16-21
Ecclesiastes 5:13-14	I Timothy 6:10
Ezekiel 7:19	I Timothy 6:17
Ezekiel 16:17	

12.   <u>Indebtedness</u>. This is still borrowing; however, this section covers specific aspects of payment and release from payment due to cancellation or forgiveness by the lender.

Genesis 38:20 There is a time element in payment of a debt.

Deuteronomy 15:1-5, 31:10-11 (release from)
II Kings 4:1, 7 (payment of)
Psalms 15:4 (payment of)
Proverbs 3:27 (payment of)

Matthew 5:25-26 (payment of)
Matthew 18:23-35 (release from) When released from a great debt remember to do likewise to those who owe you.
Luke 12:58:59 (payment of)
Romans 13:8 (payment of)
Philemon 18-19 (release from)

13. <u>Inheritance</u>. You are supposed to leave an inheritance to your children and grandchildren.

Genesis 13:15   Proverbs 13:22
Joshua 14:9   Proverbs 17:6

14. <u>Lending</u>. Do without inflicting unnecessary constraints upon the borrower.

Exodus 22:25   Psalms 112:5
Deuteronomy 15:5-6   Jeremiah 15:10
Deuteronomy 23:19   Ezekiel 18:5,7
Deuteronomy 24:10   Ezekiel 18:12,16
Deuteronomy 28:12   Luke 6:34-35
Psalms 37:25-26

15. <u>Neighbor,</u> Paying For Services Rendered. His skills and time are just as valuable as the item he's repairing/building for you. If he adamantly refuses any form of gratuity, you are not obligated.

Jeremiah 22:13   *Exodus 22:14*

16. <u>Parents,</u> Yours. Repay what you borrow from them.

Proverbs 28:24

17. <u>Partnership</u>. Do not become unequally yoked in business.

II Corinthians 6:14

18. <u>Plan</u>. God is a God of order and design. He works
by a plan; thus, He endorses sound financial planning.
      Matthew 25:27   Luke 16:1-13
      Luke 14:28

19. <u>Pleasures</u> will steal away your money.
      Proverbs 21:17

20. <u>Restitution</u>. Some financial mistakes/sins require
restitution.
      Leviticus 22:14
      Leviticus 27:30-31 (God surely gets short-
changed here; Pharaoh got 20% [the fifth part] in
taxes [Genesis 41:34, 47:24]; surely Caesar's was
higher [Matthew 17:24-27, 22:17-21] and today a 28%
tax bracket is common with stiff penalties for delin-
quency.)

21. <u>Sacrificing</u>. When you make a financial sacrifice
for others you are laying down your life for your
friend.
      Luke 10:35   Acts 4:32, 34-35

Yet, the best sacrifices are those of an anonymous
nature for God gets the glory. God sees it and will reward you accordingly.
      Job 28:10   Matthew 6:3-4
      Psalms 94:10   I Timothy 5:25, 6:17-18

22. <u>Saving</u> is wise.
      Proverbs 10:5
      Matthew 25:27

23. <u>Surety</u>; collateral; to sponsor, endorse, co-sign. It's
not wise to enter into suretyship.
      Gen 43:9, 44:32 (pledger)

D-5

Exodus 22:26 (receiver of the pledge)
Deuteronomy 24:10-13 (receiver of the pledge)
II Kings 4:1,7 (one suffering the consequences of someone else's pledge)
Job 22:6 (receiver of the pledge)
Proverbs 6:1-2 (pledger)
Proverbs 11:15 (pledger)
Proverbs 17:18 (pledger)
Proverbs 20:16 (pledger)
Proverbs 22:26-27 (pledger)
Proverbs 27:13 (pledger)

24. <u>Taxes</u>. Yes, Christians should pay taxes.
Matthew 22:19-21
Luke 20:22-25
Romans 13:7

25. <u>Tithing</u> is a commandment.

Leviticus 27:30-31
Deuteronomy 14:22
Deuteronomy 14:28-29
Deuteronomy 26:12-13
II Chronicles 31:5-8

Malachi 3:8-10
Luke 6:12
I Corinthians 16:2
Hebrew 7:1-2,4

26. <u>Usury</u>. You should not charge others interest when they borrow from you.

Exodus 22:25
Leviticus 25:35-37
Deuteronomy 23:19
Nehemiah 5:7-10

Psalms 15:5
Proverbs 28:8
Ezekiel 18:8,13
Habakkuk 2:6

(You may charge a non-Christian interest. Deuteronomy 23:20)

27. <u>Vows</u>. Any pledge, promise-to-pay or verbal financial commitment is your "word of honor". God holds you to it, even though you've made it to man.

You are accountable to God to make good that vow unless released from it by the one vowed to.

Leviticus 27:2,13	Psalms 66:13,14
Numbers 30:2	Psalms 76:11
Deu 15:1-5, 31:10-11	Proverbs 20:25
Deuteronomy 23:21-23	Ecclesiastes 5:4-6
Job 22:27	Acts 5:4
Psalms 15:4	I Timothy 5:21
Psalms 50:14	Psalms 61:8

This appendix is an extract from *Raising Responsible Children In a Single Parent Home*

Italics = new entry

WHY FAST? ISN'T PRAYING ENOUGH?

Every now and then you need to sharpen your spiritual acuity (become alert, spiritually, to the things around you) that you may know that you know that you are hearing from God and God only on a particular matter.   To accomplish this you must bring your physical drives under control, then you seek after spiritual things. Spiritual gifts will begin to operate -- the word of knowledge, word of wisdom, discernment of spirits, interpreting visions and dreams, etc. (Gen 40:8-13; Dan 1:17, 5:12,-16, and 8:16-19; and I Cor 12:8-10). Through fasting you will be able to receive spiritual things through your spiritual senses; then God will unleash spiritual power. But the Bible cautions us that this must be done in secrecy (Matt 6: 17-18).

Praying is so much a part of our spiritual lives that it's as important as breathing. We are to pray when we awaken (Ps 3:5, Prov 31:150), during the day (Dan 6;10), when we retire at night (Ps 4:8), and when God calls us to speak with us (I Sam 3:3-10). It's our telephone line, our two-way communication, with God. Yet, our Lord Jesus says some things come only by prayer and fasting (Mark 9:29). So then, the fasted prayer has the greatest affect of all for through it you enter into the upper echelons of spiritual warfare. You may be asking at this point, *"What spiritual things do I need to know about in my finances that I'll receive, wisdom, knowledge, understanding, and discernment about?"*

➡ business dealings you should not be involved with.

➡ the spiritual origin of financial situations you

may be going through.
- ➡ the root of a financial problem that's not yet revealed to you.
- ➡ knowledge of an unforeseen financial danger in your path ahead.

Before continuing further, take out time to review Isaiah 58:5-12. This way, you will have engrafted into your spirit the most important thing that the Lord has said to us about the right kind of fast prior to applying the natural things I'll share with you in the remainder of this appendix.

WHEN TO FAST

There are times when you should fast in response to spiritual guidance and when you just know you should fast.

1. You Should Fast When God Leads You To. When God led me to go on a 40 day fast I had to prepare my body and attitude as you will see later in this appendix. After I finished a 35 day fast God led me to do, He showed me, through a vision, a huge python snake, yet I had my hand so firmly around its neck that it could not move. He was showing me that the under-current in the situation I was going through was Satan, not the person he was using (Eph 6:10-12) and the way I was handling the situation gave me control over Satan in this matter (Luke 10:19, Zech 10:5).

2. You Should Fast When You Are Seeking Direction From God On A Particular Matter. When I was on the brink of preparing myself financially to maintain two children in college simultaneously, I'd decided to rent out the house and move to a small one bedroom apartment. I started looking for one yet while I looked, I fasted to seek God's wisdom on the matter. There was no set ending date. Eleven days into this absolute fast, God showed me things. In an early morning vision He showed me a bird resting in a big tree full of empty branches. He said the tree was Him and I was to rest in Him. That same morning I got up and prepared to go to work. I opened the garage door to back the car out. There was a red cardinal lying in its own blood, dead from flying into the window pane on the garage door, thinking it was an opening. God said, the bird represented me going my own way, thinking it was an opening, yet it would be fatal to me. Then the Scripture came so vividly to me, *"There is a way which seemeth right unto a man, but the end thereof are the ways of death"* (Prov 14:12).

As months passed by, one day I sat down on the sofa in the family room to read my mail. To my surprise when I looked out the patio door, the big oak tree had shed all its leaves and there it stood, big and tall, full of empty branches with a red cardinal resting in it, in my own back yard! Then I remembered the direction God spoke to me months earlier and was glad that I obeyed and stayed put in the home that He had blessed us with.

3. You Should Fast At Times Just To Sharpen Your Spiritual Alertness In What Some People May Consider "Little Things": a new friend your kids have picked up that you have a funny feeling about, a major purchase, a decision that you've got to make but you keep putting it off.

4. You Should Fast When Your Church Pastor Calls A Fast. This is a corporate time when the entire church body is spiritually empowered through unity and oneness. God calls us to be obedient to our spiritual leader. He knows when we need to come together corporately. He's only following God's guidance (Jeremiah 3:15). I've been in a Congregation where the people fasted and signed up to pray around the clock. I always got to the sign-up board late and had to pray the unpopular hours, 2:00 and 3:00 a.m. They turned out to be the most spiritually fruitful times for me.

There is much evil around us and evil is on the increase. There are even people purposely fasting for the wrong reasons. I'm not talking about weight-loss fasts. I'm talking about witchcraft users right here in America and in the church (yes, even in the church) who fast to gain evil power over churches and families (Is 58:4). Because of the unseen evil that we and our children face, we must separate ourselves from the world at times to gain wisdom, discernment and inner strength. We do this when we prayerfully fast unto the Lord Jesus Christ.

KNOW THE DIFFERENCE BETWEEN HUNGER AND APPETITE

Have you ever heard your child say, *"I'm hungry, mom"* yet you set what you have before them and they won't eat it. They're not hungry; they just have an appetite which is usually brought on by food advertised during a TV commercial, food sung about in a song, people talking about food, thinking about food, and seeing food products in magazines and the newspaper. You will have the same problem with your appetite, if you don't prepare yourself to deal with the cravings of the flesh. This is one reason why you should not watch TV or peruse any other picturesque media while fasting. Why crucify yourself with temptation as you seek after the good spiritual things? Yet, your appetite is something you can control.

An appetite is something that is spontaneous and triggered by outside sources. It stimulates your taste buds to prompt you to almost salivate over just the thought of your favorite dish. Hunger is prompted by a serious bodily need for nourishment. It causes painful sensations; a state of weakness and could lead to the onset of starvation if not satisfied. Proverbs 27:7 says, *"The full soul loatheth (tramples over) an honeycomb; but to the hungry soul every bitter thing is sweet."* In one verse further down, verse 20, we are told that, *"...the eyes of man are never satisfied."* Then Ecclesiastes 6:7 really zones in on the character of the appetite as it states, *"All the labour of man is for his mouth, and yet the appetite is not filled."* Why is this so? Because you can not satisfy a craving. It's not based on needs, but on wants. In our society, if you give a person what he wants he'll want more and more and more. An appetite is a craving and when you sense a desire for food at the beginning of your fast, relax, it's just your appetite. Buckle it under and continue with your fast.

TYPES OF FASTS

There are many Biblical scholars who label fasting types differently. These are the basic types I've found in the Bible. There are several examples but I'll just give a few:

1. Absolute Fast (No food nor water) Ex 34:28, Deu 9:18.

2. Total Fast (Water but no food) Matt 4:2, Luke 4:2.

3. No Pleasant Food Fast (Simply prepared, unpopular food item, usually eaten once, daily, with water) Dan 10:3.

4. Partial Fast (Fasted Lifestyle) (i.e., Ezekiel's grain, beans and periodic meat fast for 390 days [Ezek 4:9-15] and John the Baptist's locusts and honey diet [Matt 3:4]).

PREPARING YOUR BODY
FOR THE FAST

Now knowing that your taste buds must be bridled, prepare your body for the fast. If you are undertaking a short fast, prepare yourself Scripturally by anointing your forehead, washing your face and praying to God for His will and revelation (Matt 6:17). If you are engaging in a longer fast (For some this may be beyond a week; for others this could be from 14 - 40 days.), you need to be concerned about your eating habits 3-5 days before you begin the fast:

1. Drink only water so your body won't crave the caffeine, sugars, and tastes of commercially prepared beverages and fruit drinks.

2. Eat grain breads (whole wheat, bran, rye, barley, etc.) instead of white bread. The bulky fiber will help your bodily organs continue to function properly as you continue your daily routine.

3. Stop desserts. Some people have developed a "sweet tooth" and don't even know it. If you like desserts after almost every meal, you probably have one, too.

DURING THE FAST

Your purpose for fasting is spiritual, therefore, this time is consecrated unto the Lord. You should be reading the Bible, praying, and spending quiet time with the Lord during the times you would normally be eating. (This does not cancel out the times you should sit at the dinner table with your family with your glass of water during long fasts. Instead, this covers the other part of your three meal day and short periods of fasting.) Each day should be prayerful, all day long, with short tidbits of prayers at free moments and times of extended intercessory and spiritual warfare prayers. Concentrating on intercession for others is not only unselfish but is Scripturally good for your own spiritual growth as you learn to trust God.

You should not be consuming any other spiritual food during this time: No TV, no other media, no time on the telephone (other than business), etc. This is actually a time you've opened yourself up to the entire spiritual realm of good and evil influence, yet, you only want to hear from God. (Hopefully, after you've completed your fast and returned to TV watching you'll begin to see its ills more clearly.)

Sometimes during a long fast in which you are interceding for someone undergoing deep spiritual bondage you may experience an "appearance of sickness". I have personally experienced overcoming the flesh in this area, with much travailing.

Do purpose to get additonal rest during periods of fasting. Trying to continue the same routine with less energy will surely wear on your agility and strength. (Notice that the Lord Jesus Christ and Moses got away from the hustle and bustle to get alone with God during the entire period of their 40 days fasts. Your responsibilities may not afford you such lengthy times of seclusion from your children or job.)

During long fasts, you'll notice natural changes too. You will continue to regularly urinate; however, bowel excretion will gradually cease and will not return until you've had a "purging bowel" or have returned to eating. One time when I had been on a long term fast for eleven days without food or water, a purging came. Direction from God came later that same day. The purpose for the fast had been fulfilled; so, I ended the fast. The changes in your bodily functions during the fast should not alarm you. If you've followed the guidance above during your preparatory stage, you will have done the necessary measures it takes to sustain a sound body during this stage of the fast.

AFTER THE FAST

If you've met the time you've purposed to fast or that God has led you to fast and you have not received any direction from Him, continue to prayerfully intercede and seek His face. He will surely speak to your spirit man; you must purpose to listen and obey. (Sometimes we DO hear from God but we aren't quite sure if it's really Him because we really don't like the answer He gave.)

After an extended fast, resume food consumption slowly, with a bowl of oatmeal, soup, beans or other wholesome filler until your body can handle a full course meal without tummie queasiness. If you did not heed the advice about modifying your eating habits days before the fast begins, when you resume normal eating, you may experience pain during urination for 2-3 days. Because everyone's metabolism is different, this profile may not describe your bodily reactions to the aftermath of fasting. I've discovered this pattern to be true for me as much record keeping and repetition have been diligently considered.

After you've established a routine of leading a fasted lifestyle, you'll also begin to experience natural benefits from fasting. You'll notice

    -- a clearer complexion.

    -- healthier hair.

    -- a stronger resistance to sickness.

    -- better control over water weight gain.

    -- improved general body weight control.

    -- greater control over choosing and sticking with a good diet.

    -- alertness in your thinking.

    -- sharpened memory.

    -- sharpened taste buds.

-- cravings diminished

-- stronger control over your appetite; that is, greater control over resisting appetite stimulants which aforetime demanded your immediate gratification.

-- a strunken stomach, allowing hunger to be satisfied with less food.

-- ability to rest well at night.

-- regulated bowel movements.

-- an inner cleansing of food toxins from your system as witnessed by the following two reports. (I have no written documentation from these two references. One is from a conversation I had with a heart surgeon; the other is from a testimonial I heard over the radio.) A heart surgeon speaking at our church one day recommended that everyone should at least fast one week a year to cleanse out their system. He even said something as simple as a high pork diet can make cancer cells thrive in a stricken individual. I heard a gentleman over the radio tell of his experience in long-term fasting. He told of how at the end of one long fast he took a sample of his bowel movement to be chemically analyzed and found it full of toxin. (I really believe this to be true because of the appearance of the "bowel of purging" that occurs spontaneously when I'm weeks deep in a fast.)

We consume many chemicals and toxins, without thinking, that our body can not use for nourishment. They sit in pockets in the walls of our system and surely assist cancer cells and other health disorders to thrive with internal destruction. Long term fasting helps rid our systems of these unhealthy toxins.

Although I fast for spiritual reasons, I'm glad that these natural benefits also occur. You will also have a rewarding feeling yourself, after your fast, to know that your health has benefited that you might have the strength to continue the work of the Lord in service to your children, your church, and others around you.

When God sends His direction, you will experience the fruit of Isaiah 58:8-14 as your light breaks forth as the morning, as your health springs forth speedily, as your righteousness goes before you and the glory of the Lord covers your rear. Then, *"shalt thou call, and the Lord shall answer; thou shalt cry, and He shall say, Here I am.....and the Lord shall guide thee continually, and satisfy thy soul in drought, and make fat thy bones: and thou shalt be like a watered garden, and like a spring of water, whose waters fail not...."* and the *Lord Your God* shall cause you to, *"ride upon the high places of the earth.....for the mouth of the Lord hath spoken it."*

This appendix is an extract from *Raising Responsible Children In A Single Parent Home* (with minor changes).

E-10

APPENDIX F
AGGRESSIVE
SPIRITUAL WARFARE PRAYING
BINDING AND LOOSING

When we get so frustrated with satanic spiritual attacks from evil spirits, we begin to pray with fastings with much moaning and groaning as the Holy Spirit leads us into confronting, overpowering and then overthrowing these dark forces of the kingdom of Satan. The Lord Jesus Christ has already given us the **KEYS** of **binding** these demon forces and **loosening** the chains of darkness that hold our minds, our families, and yes, even our finances in captivity-- forces that we cannot see with the natural eye. With these KEYS, the Lord Jesus has already

> given us POWER and AUTHORITY over ALL devils.
>
> given us POWER to tread on serpents and scorpions (witchcraft, wizardry, Satanism, masonry, etc.).
>
> made the devils SUBJECT unto us.
>
> given us the ability to rescue all stolen Godgiven gifts and goods of all TRUE STEWARDS
>
> given us POWER over ALL the power of the enemy

With the massive flood of demon spirits that we have let invade our homes and churches, the Lord is calling us to come out of our passive, defensive lifestyle to that of offensive attack against these spiritual powers of darkness, for every man to *PRESS into the Kingdom of God* (enter the kingdom in spite of violent opposition), and for every man to *VIOLENTLY take the Kingdom of Heaven by force!*

God cannot quicken us to meditate, move, operate and walk in this divine anointing if we remain PASSIVE. He wants us to JOLT ourselves out of this Sluggish Stupor, this Spiritual Sleep and Slumber. With this spark in my spirit, I fervently pray that God stirs your will to earnestly covet spiritual gifts -- Spiritual Discernment, the Word of Wisdom, the Word of Knowledge and of all the Manifestation and Operational gifts you need to advance Kingdom work in the lives of others. I pray that the Lord even bestows upon YOU the Prosperity Anointing that, *"...as your hands set in motion the Scriptural principles laid out in this book, may that same Prosperity Anointing come upon your household finances and your ability to finance kingdom work for the body of Christ."*

The Spiritual Warfare prayer that follows is not an attempt to make you memorize words to quote back to God, the Father. But rather, it's an example of how you should pray when coming to the throne of God with a fervent, warfare press in your spirit man. The Lord Jesus didn't tell us to memorize the Lord's Prayer. He said, *"After this manner therefore pray ye..."* (Matt 6:9). I say to you today, just read this prayer to get this manner of violently pressing into the Kingdom of God into your spirit, then pray as God leads your spirit man. You'll find that praying for the entire Kingdom Family rather than for yourself will cause the Lord to break forth abundantly in your own life for we are all called to lift one another up in the genuine healing of pure agape love.

"SPIRITUAL WARFARE PRAYER"

COME AGAINST THE KINGDOM OF DARKNESS IN JESUS' NAME!

•Father -- Your Kingdom Come, Your Will Be Done In Earth As It Is In Heaven.

•I Hold To The Testimony Of Jesus Christ Who Is The Head Of All Principalities And Powers, In Whom Dwells All The Fullness Of The Godhead.

•I Confess All My Sins, Known & Unknown; I Ask Your Forgiveness. Cleanse Me With Your Precious Blood

•I Forgive All Others Who Have Wronged Me.

•It Is You Who Empowers Me To Engage In Spiritual Warfare Against Satan, His Principalities And Powers, His Rulers Of Darkness, His Spiritual Wickedness In High Places.

•It Is With The Authority That Jesus Has Given Me, Thru The Holy Ghost, To Use My Keys Of Authority To Bind Evil And Loose Good, That I Now Exercise My Godgiven Authority!

•I Take The Offensive And Prevail Against The Gates Of Hell In The Name Of Jesus Christ!

"BINDING"

•I Bind Specific Satanic Powers In The Earth That God May Bind Their Corresponding Principalities And Powers In The Heavenlies! In The Name Of Jesus, I Bind You!

•I Bind The Strongman! I Use My Keys Of Authority To Bind And Loose!
 ...Take Authority Over Demons!
 ...Weigh Satan Down With a Great Pile Of Chains!
 ...Use Your Authority To Bind And Loose!

•I Bind Ruler Spirits Over The Church:
 ...Bind Spirits Of Religious Pride
 False Doctrine
 Religious Traditionalism
 Superstitions
 Spirits Of Mind Control
 Spirits Of Lying, Gossip, Hindrance
 Spirits Of Fear
 Spirits Of Deception
 Spirits Of Delusion
 Spirits Of Lust

•In The Name Of Jesus Christ, I Break Your Dominion!!

•I Bind That Religious Strong Man That Promotes Division!

•Bind Witchcraft Spirits From Operating In The Church
 ...Cut Off Communication Between Witches And Demons; Bind Demon Spirits That They Cannot Interfere With Preaching, Prayers, Singers And Holy Music, Church Administration And Finances.

•In The Name Of Jesus Christ, I Command All Wicked Spirits With Specific Assignments Against My Pastor And His Family To Be Bound.

•I Command All Wicked Spirits With Specific Assignments Against Praise And Worship To Be Bound.

•I Command All Wicked Spirits With Specific Assignments Against The Choir To Be Bound.
     ... Bind Music Demons That Hinder True Worship!

•I Bind Ruler Spirits Over Denominations.

•I Bind Ruler Spirits That Separate Ethnic/Racial Groups From Worshiping God As One Family.
     ...Loose God's People, The True Remnant, To Serve God As One Body.
     ...By The Authority Given To You By The Blood Of Jesus Christ, Mightily Wrestle Against The Spiritual Powers Organized Against The True Saints. (Call Upon A Chain Of Warrior Angels To Link With You From Earth To The Heavenlies!)

•In The Name Of Jesus Christ, I Bind Ruler Spirits Coming Against Family Relationships & Finances.

•I Command Every Demon Of Curse To Get Off My Finances In The Name Of Jesus!!!

•I Bind Spirits Ruling Over Generational Curses
     Spirits of Poverty
     Spirits of Financial Insufficiency
     Spirits Of Sickness
     Spirits Of Death
     Spirits Causing Marital/Family Problems
     Spirits Of Failure In Plans, Projects, Educational Learning

• I Bind Ruler Spirits Over My City That Empower Spirits Of Crime, Lust, Greed, Witchcraft, Dishonesty, etc.

• In The Name Of Jesus Christ, I Bind Demon Spirits Which Have Been Sent Out To Hinder And Work Against The Fulfillment Of This Prayer!!!

• In The Name Of Jesus, I Declare Every Spoken Word Curse Against The Fulfillment Of This Prayer To Be Broken!
        ...Take Definite Authority Over Evil Words Spoken Against You and Confess The Blessings Of Lord God Almighty!!!

• In The Name Of Jesus Christ, I Take The KEY Of Binding That Jesus Gave To Me And Padlock It!!

• Satan, I weight Your Evil Spirits Down With A Great Pile Of Bright Golden Chains!!!

• I Cast These Wicked, Unclean Spirits Into Dry Places Where They Must Roam Aimlessly, Finding No Rest!

"LOOSING"

• In The Name Of Jesus, I Command The Chains Of The Kingdom Of Darkness To Be Loosed!

• I Loose The Bands Of The Wicked!

• I Hold The Key!! Jesus Gave It To Us!
        ...I Insert It! I Turn It!
        ...I Hear The Chains Clang As They FALL......FALL......FALL!!

• FREE...FREE...FREE!! FREE THE OPPRESSED!!
    ...Loose The Bands Of Wickedness Off The People's Hands.
    ...Break The Fetters Of Iron Off The People's Feet.
    ...Break The Fetters Of Iron Off The People's Minds.
    ...Command The Chains To Be Loosed!

• I Loose The Outpouring Of The Holy Spirit.

• I Loose The Outpouring Of Spiritual Gifts
    Discerning Of Spirits
    Words Of Knowledge
    Words Of Wisdom
    Miracles (.....i.e., Raising Of The Dead, Even From The Coffin!)
    Healings
    Prophecies
    Interpretation Of Tongues
    Divers Tongues
    (I Bind And Cast Down False Tongues)
    Ever Increasing Faith In God
    Interpretation Of Visions/Dreams
    Excellent/Extraordinary Wisdom

• By The Authority Given To Me By The Lord Jesus, I Loose The People To Mightily Operate In Their Spiritual Calling--
    Pastors
    Teachers
    Evangelists
    Prophets
    Apostles
    Ruler/Administrators
    Exhorters

Givers

Mercinaries

Entrepreneurs In Dominant/Mainstream Businesses:

    -- Major Contractors

    -- Banking/Financial Empire Owners

    -- Major Manufacturers

    -- Major Corporations

    -- Major Retail Businesses (Father God, Empower Them With Excellent And Extraordinary Wisdom!!!)

• I Loose The Power Of True Praise To The Most High God!

• I Loose The Power Of True Worship To The Most High God!

• I Plead The Redemptive Power Of The Blood Of Jesus Over Every Area I've Prayed For.

• I Live For You, LORD JESUS CHRIST

• I Glorify Your Name, Alone....

    Almighty, Omnipotent, Omnipresent, Omniscient, Holy Father

    Who Is God, For There Is None Besides You, For You Alone Are God And There Is None Else

    There Is No Other God; For You Alone Are God, Whom I Glorify, Alone

    In The Precious Name Of Your Only Begotten Son, Jesus Christ, I Pray.....A M E N.

APPENDIX-G
TRANSPARENCY MASTERS
for
GROUP INSTRUCTION

This appendix consists of Transparency Masters (for Parts I & II of this book) which can be used in any group setting in church, at home, on your job and in your community to spread the word about God's foundational principles on money management. These Transparency Masters can be used by anyone who desires to share with others God's spiritual and natural disciplines in successful family resource management. The Lord Jesus admonished Peter that to show his love for Him he must *"feed my lambs"* (referring to individual, one-on-one nurturing) and *"feed my sheep"* (referring to the nurture of a group, as a congregational setting). I, too, heed the call to nurture the flock of God and pray that any Christian leader that picks up this book also picks up this spirit of obedience to the commission our Lord Jesus gave to all who are true disciples of Christ.

I must warn you that this is a very spiritual book. It will totally defeat your purpose of educating others and prospering yourself if you violate the copyright laws. All students should purchase individual copies of this book as a family financial resource reference that supplements their family Bible. Students are then at liberty to copy any forms needed to execute the disciplines contained herein.

NOTE: Masters have been reduced to 78%. Enlarge by 22% to obtain full-sized pages.

FOR MEN ONLY!!!

CAN I _TRUST_ MY WIFE AS THE FINANCIAL BUDGET KEEPER?

THE BIBLE SAYS, YES!!!!

Genesis 2:18, 20
STRONG's **#5828 Heb *"ezer"* -- aid; help; succour**

HELP-MEET → HELP-MATE → WIFE

WEBSTER'S/WORLD BOOK
surround; succor; promote
to change for the better
remedy; relief; support
to relieve and assist in time of want, need, danger,
trouble, or distress

THE TRUTH ABOUT "BUDGET PLANS"

A BUDGET PLAN IS FOR A FAMILY WHO

- WANTS TO BE ORGANIZED
- WANTS TO KNOW WHERE THEIR MONEY GOES
- WANTS TO DRIVE AT NITE WITH THEIR HEADLIGHTS ON
- WANTS TO BE ACCT'BLE TO GOD FOR STEWARDSHIP
- SEES A ROAD MAP.....
    - A WAY OF ARRIVING AT THEIR DESTINATION (=financial freedom)
    - AT THE EARLIEST TIME (= early payoff)
    - USING THE LEAST AMOUNT OF GAS (= least $ on %)
    - W/ THE LEAST AMOUNT OF WEAR & TEAR (= ignorant decisions, $ sins, $ curses, repeatedly starting over & over again...)
    - ON THEIR AUTO (= their means of making $)

Discipline In Family Resource Management

Planning Your Family Budget

		INTERIM	IDEAL
1.	Tithes	X	X
2.	Mortg	X	X
3.	Car Ins	X	X
4.	Car Rpr/Maint	X	X
5.	Church Offerings	X	X
6.	Othr Dona/Giv	X	X
7.	Gas	X	X
8.	Phone	X	X
8.	Electric	X	X
8.	Water	X	X
8.	Heating Oil	X	X
8.	Grocery	X	X
9.	Consumer Debt	X	X
10.	Car Note	X	X
11.	Life Ins (Extra)		X
12.	Savings		X
13.	Lunch $		X
14.	Allowances		X
15.	Garbage		X
16.	Cable		X
17.	Eat-Out		X
18.	Vacation		X

CLEARING THE AIR ON.....

- GIVING OUTSIDE THE CHURCH (ACTS 11:28-30)

- GIVING IN NON-DOLLAR AREAS: TIME & SKILL

- THE 3 AREAS OF CHURCH GIVING IDENTIFIED IN THE BIBLE
  -- TITHES
  -- OFFERINGS
  -- VOWS & PLEDGES

- INCREASE: IS ALL INCOME NECESSARILY INCREASE???
  -- "RENT" MONEY RECEIVED FROM LIVE-IN FAMILY MEMBERS APPLIED TO BUDGET EXPENSES
  --TAX REFUND
  --INSURANCE REIMBURSEMENT ON LOSSES

THE 1ST STEP IN MAKING YOUR BUDGET WORK "REPENTANCE FOR FINANCIAL SINS"

- THAT *THAT* WHICH IS GOD'S S/N BE TAKEN FROM US & GIVEN TO ANOTHER (Matt 25:27-30)

- THAT WE MIGHT STOP WEEPING & GNASHING OUR TEETH

- THAT WE MIGHT FLEE YOUTH LUSTS (II Tim 2:22)

- THAT WE MIGHT NOT CONTINUE TO OPPOSE OURSELVES (II Tim 2:25)

- THAT WE MIGHT RECOVER OURSELVES OUT OF THE SNARE OF THE DEVIL, WHO HAS TAKEN US CAPTIVE (II Tim 2:26)

"MY DESIRE IS THAT I'VE INSTRUCTED YOU IN MEEKNESS THAT YOUR FINANCIAL MANAGEMENT SKILLS MIGHT BECOME SPIRITUALLY EMPOWERED"
BE BLESSED IN THE LORD JESUS!!!

References

Britt, Viola L., *Raising Responsible Children In A Single Parent Home*, Kirkwood, Missouri, Impact Christian Books, 1997

Britt, Viola L., *Family Planner - Companion Workbook to Discipline In Family Resource Management*, Kirkwood, Missouri, Impact Christian Books, 1998

Barton, David, *America's Godly Heritage*, Aledo, Texas, Wallbuilders, 1990

Strong's Exhaustive Concordance of the Bible, Virginia, MacDonald Publishing Co.

Vine's Complete Expository Dictionary of Old and New Testament Words, Nashville, Thomas Nelson Publishers, 1984

Webster Encyclopedic Unabridged Dictionary of the English Language, New York, Gramercy Books, 1989

The World Book Dictionary, Doubleday & Co., 1975

Song:
Leech, Lida S., *Trust, Try, and Prove Me*, ©1923, renewal 1951, Broadman Press

—Ministry and personal inquiries to:—

Speak Holy Spirit
Ministry
P.O. Box 11312
Goldsboro, N.C. 27532-1312

§

"For it is not ye that speak, but the Spirit of your Father which speaketh in you...What I tell you in darkness, that speak ye in light: and what ye hear in the ear, that preach ye upon the housetops." St. Matthew 10:20, 27

A BLOOD COVENANT
IS THE MOST
SOLEMN, BINDING AGREEMENT POSSIBLE
BETWEEN TWO PARTIES.

Perhaps one of the least understood, and yet most important and relevant factors necessary for an appreciation of the series of covenants and covenant relationships that our God has chosen to employ in His dealings with man, is the concept of the BLOOD COVENANT!

In this volume which has been "sold out," and "unavailable" for generations, lies truth which has blessed and will continue to bless every pastor, teacher, every serious Christian desiring to "go on with God."

Andrew Murray stated it beautifully years ago, when he said that if we were to but grasp the full knowledge of what God desires to do for us and understood the nature of His promises, it would "make the Covenant the very gate of heaven! May the Holy Spirit give us some vision of its glory."

$10.95 + 2.00 postage and handling

THE HEAVENS DECLARE . . .

William D. Banks

More than 250 pages!
More than 50 illustrations!

- Who named the stars and why?
- What were the original names of the stars?
- What is the secret message hidden in the stars?

The surprising, **secret message** contained in the earliest, original names of the stars, is revealed in this new book.

The deciphering of the star names provides a fresh revelation from the heart of **the intelligence** behind creation. Ten years of research includes material from the British Museum dating prior to 2700 B.C.

A clear explanation is given showing that early man had a sophisticated knowledge of One, True God!

$6.95 + $1.50 Shipping/Handling

ALIVE AGAIN!

William D. Banks

The author, healed over twenty years ago, relates his own story. His own testimony presents a miracle or really a series of miracles — as seen through the eyes of a doubting skeptic, who himself becomes the object of the greatest miracle, because he is Alive Again!

The way this family pursues and finds divine healing as well as a great spiritual blessing provides a story that will at once bless you, refresh you, restore your faith or challenge it! You will not be the same after you have read this true account of the healing gospel of Jesus Christ, and how He is working in the world today.

The healing message contained in this book needs to be heard by every cancer patient, every seriously ill person, and by every Christian hungering for the reality of God.

More than a powerful testimony — here is teaching which can introduce you or those whom you love to healing and to a new life in the Spirit!

$4.95 + $1.50 Shipping/Handling

POWERFUL NEW BOOK

This new book is unique because it offers real help for the suffering women who have already had abortions. This book is full of GOOD NEWS!

It shows how to minister to them, or may be used by the women themselves as it contains simple steps to self-ministry.

Millions of women **have had abortions**: every one of them is a potential candidate for the type of ministry presented in this book. Every minister, every counsellor, every Christian should be familiar with these truths which can set people free.

$5.95 + $1.50 Shipping/Handling

Impact Christian Books, Inc.
332 Leffingwell Avenue, Suite 101
Kirkwood, MO 63122

This book was a favorite of the late Kathryn Kuhlman who often read from it on her radio show.

Early Church Writers such as Justin refer to the existence of these records, and Tertullian specifically mentions the report made by Pilate to the Emperor of Rome, Tiberius Caesar.

Chapters Include:
- *How These Records Were Discovered,*
- *A Short Sketch of the Talmuds,*
- *Constantine's Letter in Regard to Having Fifty Copies of the Scriptures Written and Bound,*
- *Jonathan's Interview with the Bethlehem Shepherds   Letter of Melker, Priest of the Synagogue at Bethlehem,*
- *Gamaliel's Interview with Joseph and Mary and Others Concerning Jesus,*
- *Report of Caiaphas to the Sanhedrim Concerning the Resurrection of Jesus,*
- *Valleus's Notes — "Acta Pilati," or Pilate's Report to Caesar of the Arrest, Trial, and Crucifixion of Jesus,*
- *Herod Antipater's Defense Before the Roman Senate in Regard to His Conduct At Bethlehem,*
- *Herod Antipas's Defense Before the Roman Senate in Regard to the Execution of John the Baptist,*
- *The Hillel Letters Regarding God's Providence to the Jews, by Hillel the Third*

THE ACTS OF PILATE $9.95, plus $2.00 Shipping

IMPACT CHRISTIAN BOOKS, INC.
332 Leffingwell Ave., Suite 101, Kirkwood, MO 63122

EXCITING NEW BOOK
ANSWERS AGE-OLD QUESTION

The author draws upon the Scriptural patterns and keys established by the Prophet Daniel to present readily understandable methods any believer can employ to *Tap into the Wisdom of God*. He shows from Scripture that it is both God's intention and will for man to turn to Him as the Source of knowledge.

You will learn seven major keys to receiving knowledge and find at least twenty-one practical encouragements to build your faith to seek God for answers.

Plus a Revelation

Discover for yourself the fascinating and prophetic secrets contained in Daniel Chapter Six, presented in the ninth chapter of this book. Chapter nine, which is actually a bonus book, presents an apparently undiscovered revelation showing more than one hundred parallels between Daniel and Jesus Christ.

"The most exciting thing I discovered was that what God did for Daniel, He can do for any believer!"

P.M., Bible Teacher, Kansas.

$10.95 + $1.50 Shipping

Impact Christian Books, Inc.
332 Leffingwell Ave., Suite 101,
Kirkwood, MO 63122

332 Leffingwell Ave., Suite 101
Kirkwood, MO 63122

AVAILABLE AT YOUR LOCAL BOOKSTORE, OR YOU MAY
ORDER DIRECTLY. Toll-Free, order-line only M/C, DISC,
or VISA 1-800-451-2708.

Write for *FREE* Catalog.